# IT IS FINISHED

# IT IS FINISHED

*Meditations on the Death of Jesus*

DARRELL W. JOHNSON

REGENT COLLEGE PUBLISHING
Vancouver, British Columbia

Published 2008 by Regent College Publishing
5800 University Boulevard, Vancouver, BC V6T 2E4 Canada
Web: www.regentpublishing.com
E-mail: info@regentpublishing.com

Regent College Publishing is an imprint of the Regent
Bookstore <www.regentbookstore.com>. Views expressed in
works published by Regent College Publishing are those of the
author and do not necessarily represent the official position of
Regent College <www.regent-college.edu>.

Unless otherwise noted, Scripture taken from the New
American Standard Bible, © Copyright 1960, 1962, 1963,
1968, 1971, 1972, 1973, 1975, 1977, 1995 by the Lockman
Foundation. Used by permission. Uppercase pronouns for
deity have been maintained in quotations from the NASB in
observance of copyright law.

Library and Archives Canada Cataloguing in Publication

Johnson, Darrell W., 1947–
It is Finished : Meditations on the Death of Jesus /
Darrell W. Johnson.

Includes bibliographical references.
ISBN-10: 1-57383-401-7
ISBN-13: 978-1-57383-401-8

1. Jesus Christ—Crucifixion—Sermons. 2. Holy Cross—
Sermons. I. Title.

BT453.J53 2008                    232.96'3
C2007-906209-1

# CONTENTS

# PREFACE

A t the centre of the Christian Story stands a Person and an Event. The Person, Jesus of Nazareth; the Event, His death by crucifixion on a Roman cross.

In these pages, I am inviting you to go back with me to that Friday afternoon, March 23, 33 A.D., when the carpenter from Galilee was executed in a manner reserved for the most degrading and despised in Roman society.[1] I know the cross is no longer there. I know that He is no longer dead. But because what happened that afternoon stands at the centre of the Christian understanding of history, I invite you to go back with me, and to the best of your ability, imagine standing on that hill close enough to see and hear and smell. Look. Listen. Feel. Think. Take in as much of that horrific event as you are able. Hear the cynical crowd yell, "He saved others; can He not save Himself?"

---

1.  See Michael Green, *The Empty Cross of Jesus* (Downers Grove, Ill.: InterVarsity Press), 1984, 21-23.

Yes, He can. But that is not what He came to do. The question: would we have understood what was happening? Had we stood there with Mary Magdalene, Mary the mother of Jesus, John, and other frightened and grieving followers, would we have understood what was happening?

Had we been unaware of the things Jesus said and did, we might have concluded that He, like the other two men hanging beside Him, was a criminal getting what He deserved. Had we heard the rumor that He claimed to be the long-awaited Jewish Messiah, we might have concluded that what was happening to Him is what happens to all misguided messianic figures. Had we known that He was a good man, that He had done nothing wrong, we might have concluded that here is yet another example of how unjust human legal systems can be. If we had encountered Him along the way, and seen for ourselves how much He loved God and sought to do the godly thing, we might have concluded, bitterly so, that here was another indication that God does not seem to be able to do anything about the suffering of the innocent. If we had been able to get near the cross and watch how He treated those who were crucifying Him; if we had heard Him pray, "Father, forgive them for they do not know what they are doing"; if we had been able to get close enough to catch a glimpse of His eyes, eyes filled with compassion for the soldiers standing guard, we might have concluded that although this Man of Love would die, His example would not. And we might have even decided to give ourselves to that example and follow in His steps.

But would we have understood what was really happening? Would we have concluded what the authors of the New Testament later came to grasp and proclaim? Would we have understood that this is the central event of history? That this is the pivotal event of God's history?

The Gospel writers tell us that from the sixth hour until the ninth (from noon until three in the afternoon) "darkness came over all the land." Why? The first three Gospel writers (Matthew, Mark and Luke) tell us that toward the end of those three hours Jesus cried out in a loud voice, "My God, My God, why have You forsaken Me?" Why indeed? The fourth Gospel writer John tells us that just before He breathed His last, Jesus said, "It is finished!" (John 19:30).

What is finished?

That is the question, the million-dollar question: What is finished? What is done that never needs to be done again? What is completed, to which no one ever need add a thing? It is not only an interesting theological question; it turns out to be one of the most practical questions we can ever ask. For the longer we stand beneath the cross, the more we realize that we desperately need to have happen what happened. And either we believe that it has happened—it is finished—or we will spend the rest of our lives trying to make it happen ourselves.

What is finished?

Something ultimate, in every sense of the word. Something final, in every sense of the word. Something cosmic, literally cosmic.

You have in your hands six sermons on the cross of Jesus. I have not tried to change these sermons from their oral form to written form. So, for example, I have kept clauses that serve as sentences. I have tired to take out oral devices like repetition, crucial for the ear but potentially irritating to the eye. I hope that as you read these words with you eyes you will end up hearing them with your ears. Martin Luther once said, "Faith is an acoustical affair."[2] He regularly exhorted the people he served to "stick your eyes in your ears." In the nature of things we see through the ear; we look by listening.

Think of these six sermons as six perspectives on the cross. There are many more! No single perspective exhausts the meaning of Jesus' death. In these six sermons I offer six perspectives that I think take us to the heart of the event. Think of them as six windows through which we can discover the core achievements of Jesus' willing sacrifice on the cross. As you look through each window I pray that you will come to a deep, deep awareness and conviction that what was done there was done for you, and for the world. And I pray that you will come to believe at the deepest level of your being, that what was done none of us ever needs to do; everything that needs to be done *is* done! And I pray that you and I will then live into the freedom and joy and fullness such awareness and conviction brings.

I have preached various forms of each of the six sermons in all kinds of different cultural contexts, from California to the Philippines to Canada to Sweden. And every time, both I who preached and those who heard were moved to the core of our beings by the incredibly good news of Good Friday.

I want to acknowledge the assistance of three of my Teaching Assistants. David Lee typed the manuscript from my bits and pieces of preaching notes, and turned some of my idiosyncratic oral rhetorical devices into clearer written communication. David Williams helped me run down the sources of quotations and then took a group of young guys through the sermons, getting their feedback on the exposition of the texts. Aaron Roberts combed the manuscript making helpful corrections. And I want to thank

---

2.  Quoted by Richard Lisher, *A Theology of Preaching* (Nashville: Abingdon, 1981), p. 70.

Rob Clements, editor of Regent College Publishing for his always careful, precise feedback on my work. Any remaining errors are, of course, mine.

Finished. Done. Complete.

What is finished?

Come, and see.

CHAPTER ONE

# THE JUSTIFICATION
# OF GRACE

*Romans 3:21-26*

The person who has most helped the world begin to understand what happened that Friday afternoon is the apostle Paul, the former Saul of Tarsus, a brilliant rabbi of the first century. At first he was put off by the cross and what the first disciples where claiming about the cross. Paul, along with many others, initially simply concluded that Jesus had to be a cursed man. In the Old Testament book Deuteronomy, Paul and the others read, "Cursed is everyone who hangs on a tree" (21:23). But the more he looked, and listened, and thought, the more things were opened up to him, things were revealed to him. And he came to understand what he could never have figured out on his own.

So let us begin with "The Apostle of the Cross" as he is sometimes called. Imagine him standing with us on the hill outside Jerusalem. Imagine us turning to him and asking, "Paul, what do you understand to be taking place?" Oh my!

And let us begin with a densely packed text he wrote to the believers in Rome. The text is Romans 3:21-26. In it the apostle takes us to the very heart of the finished work of the crucified Lord. Through these theologically loaded (!) verses, we are drawn into the deepest depths of Jesus' work on the cross.

The key line of the text is "This was to demonstrate His righteousness" (v. 25). "For a demonstration, I say, of His righteousness" (v. 26). The apostle of the cross says it twice because therein lies the most fundamental achievement of the death of Jesus Christ. "This was to demonstrate His righteousness", or as the New International Version renders it, "He did this to demonstrate His justice."

We ask of the text, Who is the "He"? The Living God. We ask, Whose righteousness, whose justice, is being demonstrated? The Living God's. And we ask, What is the "this" which demonstrates the righteousness/justice of God? "Jesus Christ publicly displayed as a propitiation" (vs. 25).

What is Paul, the former rabbi, getting at in using these words, phrases and images?

Romans 3:21-26

21 But now apart from the Law the righteousness of God has been manifested, being witnessed by the Law and the Prophets,

22 even the righteousness of God through faith in Jesus Christ for all those who believe; for there is no distinction;

23  for all have sinned and fall short of the glory of God,

24  being justified as a gift by His grace through the redemption which is in Christ Jesus;

25  whom God displayed publicly as a propitiation in His blood through faith. This was to demonstrate His righteousness, because in the forbearance of God He passed over the sins previously committed;

26  for the demonstration, I say, of His righteousness at the present time, that He might be just and the justifier of the one who has faith in Jesus.

In his letter to the Romans, Paul is dealing with the nature of the relationship between unholy humanity and the Holy God. The Greek term translated "justice" in the second half of the text and "righteousness" in the first half, is the same term. And it is a relational term. It's root meaning is "faithfulness to a relationship," that is, "right relationship." A person is "righteous" or "just" who lives up to the terms and expectations of a relationship. Thus a citizen is called "righteous" or "just" who lives up to what the nation expects of its citizens. A spouse is "righteous" or "just" who lives up to the terms of the marriage covenant. The primary relationship of life is between a human being and the Living God. A person who has lived up to the terms of that relationship is in right standing; he or she is "righteous", and "justified."

In his letter to the Romans Paul is wrestling with two facts of history.

Fact one: *None of us, in and of ourselves, is righteous before God.* In Romans 3:10, Paul quotes the Psalmist who laments, "There is none righteous, not even one."

15

No human being,[1] however good or noble, has lived up to God's expectations. Those who claim they have, simply have not understood who God is and what God expects. Who can hear God's Law, the Ten Commandments, and say, "Dude! Like, that totally describes my life"? Who can read through the Sermon on the Mount and afterwards say, "That's me all right, I embody that 'exceeding righteousness' Jesus describes"? As Paul says in our text, "All have sinned and fall short of the glory of God" (3:23). *All.*

Fact one: *No human in and of him or herself, has been or is righteous before God.*

Fact two: *The Living God is all-together righteous, all-together just.* The Holy God has consistently lived up to the terms of all of God's relationships.

Or has God? Has the Living God been faithful to the relationship with God's own Self? In particular, has the Living God been faithful to God's own Holiness? If God has not, then we have to also ask, has God really been faithful to the terms of God's relationship with us?

You see, apart from the cross event, it appears that God is not righteous, that God is not just. Take note of the phrase, "Because in the forbearance of God He passed over the sins previously committed," or as the *NIV* has it, "because in God's forbearance God had left the sins committed beforehand unpunished" (3:25). The apostle Paul recognized that since that day when the first humans sinned, since the fall of humanity, God has not dealt with human sin in the way God's character demands.

Only on a few occasions, like the flood in Noah's day, and the destruction of Sodom and Gomorrah in Abraham's day, has God dealt with us as God ought.

---

1. Other than Jesus of Nazareth, of course.

Why do I say that? Because the Living God is Holy. Holiness is the essence of the Divine Being. "Holy, Holy, Holy," sing the angelic hosts who dwell in God's unveiled presence.

Here is the problem: Holiness, by its very nature, reacts against all that is not holy. That is putting it mildly! Holiness recoils against and seeks to burn away all that is not holy. Yet Paul says, "In the forbearance of God He passed over the sins previously committed." History seems to indicate that the Holy God has not acted in ways God's Holiness demands. It appears, therefore, that the Living God has not been righteous, has not been just.

The problem is heightened by the Incarnation, by the way the Holy One-made-flesh acts on earth. Jesus, who can say, "They who have seen Me have seen the Father" (John 14:9), freely relates to unholy people just as they are! Again and again the charge was leveled against Jesus: "This man welcomes sinners and eats with them" (Luke 15:2). The religious authorities said these words out of disgust and horror.

The problem is further heightened by the way Jesus responded to their charge. To explain His actions Jesus tells His most famous parable, the parable of the Prodigal Son or as it should be called, the Parable of the Prodigal Sons (Luke 15) since it is about two brothers. The father in Jesus' story freely welcomes back the younger son who has squandered one-third of the family wealth and shamed the family name. When the father in the story sees the wayward, that is, unrighteous, son coming home he runs to meet him, throwing his arms around him. The father accepts the son just as he is, filthy rags and all, and then throws a party in the unrighteous son's honor!

Jesus is saying that this is how the Living God treats unholy people who turn around and come home. The Holy One welcomes us with open arms, and embraces us while we are still unholy. As Paul puts it in our text, God justifies us, that is, makes us right with God's self by grace, solely on the basis of God's free decision to pardon us. God justifies me as a gift; it is, as Billy Graham says, "just as if I'd never sinned."

That is wonderful and liberating news! But it is often so hard to believe. All we need to do is "come home" and we will be welcomed? Then why does it take so long for that Good News to affect our everyday living? Partly because of our pride, we want to be able to say, "I made it on my own." But mostly because there is a deeply rooted sense that God cannot let us off that easily, that something more ought to be done. There is this sense that in freely justifying us God has ignored or violated something.

The older son in Jesus' parable is actually angry that the younger son gets to come home no questions asked. His anger is not just sibling jealousy. The older son is angry because everything the father in the story does is scandalous; everything the father does calls into question the father's righteousness.[2] As far as the older son is concerned, the father is acting unrighteously.

This is precisely the issue with which the apostle Paul is wrestling. Throughout history, the Holy God has dealt with humanity mercifully, even graciously. God has "passed over sins," not treating sins as God's essential character demands. In fact, God has gone to the other extreme, so to speak, and freely brought us unholy ones into relationship. God acquits by grace and makes us righteous as a gift. If governments treated lawbreakers the way God treats us there would be utter chaos. "In God's forbearance God had left the sins committed beforehand unpunished."

---

2. See Dr. Kenneth Bailey, *The Cross and the Prodigal* (Downers Grove, Ill.: InterVarsity Press), 2005.

Let us dig a bit deeper. By relating to us in grace, it appears that God is doing a number of troublesome things. First, it appears that God is condoning our sin, that sin makes no difference to God. That is why the Pharisees, the self appointed protectors of God's reputation, had such trouble with Jesus, the supposed Righteous One, eating and drinking with tax collectors and prostitutes. Jesus appeared to condone their sin. Second, it appears that God is mocking us. As New Testament scholar Charles Cranfield notes, it appears that God does not respect us as morally accountable creatures. "Hey, it's no big deal. Boys will be boys, girls will be girls." Third, and most critically, it appears that God is compromising God's own character. When the Holy One freely brings us unholy sinners into relationship, it appears that God is denying who God is.

We, in our time ask: "How can God be good if God does not accept everyone?" But, the question that *biblical authors* ask is: "How can God be God if God accepts anyone?"

Our sin and God's essential character create a huge problem for us, but also for God. God's essential character demands that something be done. But what? Dr. Vernon Grounds expresses the dilemma best:

> In God's holiness God cannot wink at sin, pretending it does not matter. God cannot lightly pardon humanity's guilty disobedience. No, God's justice requires that the sinner be punished. And that punishment is nothing less or other than death. And yet to send humanity into eternal exile would mean the frustration of God's very purpose in creating the creature . . . So what can God do? Blot out the blunder and stand forever baffled in the fulfillment of His desire by the will of a mere creature?[3]

---

3. Vernon Grounds, "God's Perspective on Man" *JASA* 28 (Dec. 1976), 145-151.

God's essential character ought to respond to our sin in anger —in holy anger. We have destroyed His good work. God's essential character ought to respond in judgment. The Holy One would be perfectly just, all together righteous to act toward us in wrath. In fact, to do so would demonstrate His righteousness. Unless we accept that fact we will never understand the cross.

How do you respond to the word "wrath"? For most people the word conjures up a picture of someone in a fit of rage who is out of control. Thank God that his wrath is not like that! The wrath of God is a controlled, but relentless, righteous reaction to anything unrighteous.

Dr. Leon Morris of Australia has done some of the best work on the concept of wrath. He writes: "The wrath of God is often (wrongly) confused with that irrational passion we so frequently find in man and which was commonly ascribed to heathen deities."[4] He goes on to say that God's wrath "denotes not so much a sudden flaring up of passion which is soon over, as a strong and settled opposition to all that is evil, [an opposition] arising out of God's very nature."[5] God's wrath "is a burning zeal for the right coupled with a perfect hatred for everything that is evil."[6]

Throughout the ages human beings have implicitly known this, and they have implicitly known the problem it creates for the Living God's desire to have a relationship with sinful human beings. This is why we find in nearly every culture throughout the ages myths about angry gods whose anger needs to be averted, usually by a human sacrifice.

---

4.  Leon Morris, *The Apostolic Preaching of the Cross* (London: The Tyndale Press), 1965, 130.

5.  Ibid., 162-163.

6.  Ibid., 181.

Ever since living in the Philippines,[7] I have been working with a presupposition. It is this: The myths of ancient and modern cultures are in touch with fundamental truths. The myths often distort these fundamental truths, in some cases grossly so. But the myths usually contain some residue of fundamental truth, which God has placed within the human spirit and conscience.

So, for example, nearly every ancient culture around the globe has a myth about a great flood which engulfed the earth. Why? Because there was a great flood. Nearly every ancient (and modern) culture has a myth about evil spirits, usually distorted into ghosts and goblins. Why? Because there is more to evil than bad human choices; there are evil spiritual powers. Many ancient (and modern) cultures have myths about extra-terrestrial beings coming to earth, to bring earthlings resources they do not have in themselves. "Superman" and "E.T." are 20th century versions of the myth. Why this universal longing for a rescuer from outside this world? Because, as a matter of fact, our only hope is for someone from outside the prison to come and set the prisoners free! And, nearly every culture has myths about angry gods needing to be appeased. Why? Because as we learn from God's self-revelation in Scripture, the One, True and Living God is not neutral in the face of sin and evil. The Living God, who is "Holy, Holy, Holy," ought to be angry with the world. God would not be righteous; God would not be just if God were not angry. A wrath-less God is a care-less God. A wrath-less God is a love-less God. A wrath-less God is a justice-less God.

So what is God to do?

**"God did this to demonstrate His righteousness."**

Did what? Verse 25:

---

7.   1985-1989.

"Presented Jesus Christ as a propitiation."

*Propitiation*. It is a word which many of us would rather avoid and thereby miss out on the heart of the cross, the heart of the Good News. "To propitiate" means "to appease, to pacify, to avert the anger of another," usually by a peace offering. Here is the Good News: in the death of Jesus, in the shed blood of Jesus, the Holy One has propitiated holy wrath!

Some Christian scholars argue that the word Paul uses should not be translated "propitiation" but "expiation," and thus argue we should render Paul's words: "God presented Jesus Christ as an expiation." To "expiate" means to cover over, to put away, to rub out. It is argued that in the death of Jesus Christ God has covered over sin, has taken it away, has rubbed it out, so that our sin no longer presents a problem to God, and God is then free to relate to us in mercy and grace.

As a matter of fact, the death of Jesus Christ does expiate our sin. As the scapegoat did in the Old Testament sacrificial system, so Jesus the Lamb of God does — He takes away the sin of the world! But that is not the heart of the cross event. "Expiation means only half of what propitiation means."[8] God is so holy that God cannot even look at sin to cover it without first dealing with His holy anger. "God did this to demonstrate God's justice." At the cross God did what the Divine character demands — God propitiated righteous wrath.

It is critical to note that this act is very different from pagan ideas. For one thing, God's anger is not like the anger of the god of the myths. It is not irrational, arbitrary or vindictive. More critically, it is God who takes the initiative in propitiating wrath.

---

8.   J. I. Packer, *Knowing God* (Downers Grove, Ill.: InterVarsity Press, 1973), 163.

God does not wait for humanity to offer a sacrifice to avert God's anger. Rather God offers the sacrifice—the sacrifice of the God-Man, Jesus of Nazareth.

And therein lies another difference from pagan ideas—a crucial difference. The sacrifice which averts God's wrath is God's Son, no one else's. God never demanded the sacrifice of human children as the myths teach because all along God intended to offer the only begotten Son. The myths were right that something needed to be done; they were wrong about what that something was.

"God did this . . . " God sent the only begotten Son into the world to become one of us. But more than just one of us. God sent the Son to become the "Representative Human being." Pontius Pilate placed the sign on the cross, which read: "Jesus of Nazareth, King of the Jews." But, as a number of commentators have suggested, had God placed a sign on the cross it would have read: "Jesus of Nazareth, the whole human race." And then, in those three terrifying hours the Representative Human being bore the righteous wrath of the Righteous God.

This is why Jesus agonized in the Garden the night before: "Oh Father, let this cup pass from Me." The cup was the cup of wrath. That is why as Jesus hung on the cross darkness fell across the whole land. Darkness is the sign of judgment. That is why He cries out, "My God, My God, why has Thou forsaken Me?"

"God did this to demonstrate God's righteousness." God's holiness demanded a sacrifice; God's love provided it![9]

Again, lest we think this is too pagan, remember Who the sacrifice is. The Son is no third party between God and

---

9.    Traditionally attributed to 18th century Baptist preacher Augustus Strong.

23

humanity. The Son is God! Jesus is the Eternal Word made flesh, the Creator become a human being. Jesus is Immanuel, God-with-us, Yahweh-Himself-to-the-rescue. Which means that at the cross God expresses His Holy wrath against Himself!

And then cries out, "It is finished." All done. Satisfied forever.

Therefore, when the Holy God accepts us just as we are, God is not condoning our sin. When the Holy God takes us into the Family, just as we are, God is not mocking us, ignoring moral accountability. When the Holy God embraces us in Jesus with both arms, God is not compromising the Divine Character. God did what God's character demands at the cross. All that needs to be done has been done by God, to God. At the cross (as John Stott puts it) God Himself saved us from Himself. Or, as I want to put it, at the cross God Himself saves us from Himself for Himself.

The universe is on firm footing. Grace has been justified!

And all we need do now is throw ourselves into the arms of this God, offering ourselves as living sacrifices (Romans 12:1-2).

> Amazing love, how can it be,
> That Thou my God, shouldst die for me?

Who could have ever dreamed up such a God? All praise be unto Him both now and forever.

Finished!

# CHAPTER TWO

# THE RANSOM THAT SETS US FREE

*Mark 10:45; 1 Timothy 2:5-6*

What is it that explains the magnetic power of the cross of Jesus? Why does His cross, "the emblem of suffering and shame" as the old hymn puts it, tug at the human soul the way it does?

From all appearances the crucifixion of Jesus of Nazareth is a weak and foolish event; indeed, from all appearances it is a failure, a total defeat. Yet, nearly everyone who stands beneath the cross of Jesus, literally or figuratively, implicitly knows that there is more going on there, and is drawn in by that *more*. As George Bennard sings in that old hymn (1913),

> O that old rugged cross, so despised by the world,
> Has a wondrous attraction to me."

Why? Why "a wondrous attraction"? This is so even in the soul of unbelievers. Take Malcolm Muggeridge, the famous commentator of the British Broadcast Company, for instance. Raised in a socialist family, the only Jesus he knew was what he calls "the Jesus of good causes." Yet, as he shares in his book *Jesus Rediscovered*, the cross strangely pulled at him. He writes:

> I would catch a glimpse of a cross—not necessarily a crucifix; maybe two pieces of wood accidentally nailed together, on a telegraph pole, for instance—and suddenly my heart would stand still. In an instinctive, intuitive way I understood that something more important, more tumultuous, more passionate, was at issue than our good causes, however admirable they might be . . . [1]

Why does the cross, "the emblem of suffering and shame," tug at the human soul the way it does?

> For even the Son of Man did not come to be served, but to serve, and to give His life a ransom for many. (Mark 10:45)

> For there is one God, and one mediator also between God and men, the man Christ Jesus, who gave Himself as a ransom for all, the testimony borne at the proper time. (1 Timothy 2:5-6)

In Mark 10:45 Jesus gives us His own interpretation of His crucifixion. "The Son of Man"—Jesus' favorite self-designation—"came not to be served, but to serve, and to give His life a ransom for many." Some thirty years later, the apostle Paul echoes Jesus' words: " . . . the Man Christ Jesus, who gave Himself as a ransom."

The Greek word translated "ransom" ("*lutron*") is the root word of a whole cluster of words used in connection with the cross

---

1. Malcolm Muggeridge, *Jesus Rediscovered* (London: Fontana), 1969, 24.

of Jesus; words like "redeem," "redemption," "redemptive," and "redeemer."

Although the Church has employed this cluster of words for centuries—our hymns and preaching are saturated with them—the Church has done so uncritically. That is, the cluster of words —"ransom," "redeems," "redemption"—has come to have a very wide range of meanings; they serve as vague synonyms for words like "save" and "salvation." And this is most unfortunate, for in the first century these words had a very precise meaning.

Leon Morris argued that this word group does not mean salvation in general, but a particular kind of salvation.[2] Morris pointed out that whereas we in our century hear the words and immediately think in religious terms, people of the first century heard them and "immediately thought in non-religious terms." "Indeed," he writes, "that was the reason the words came to be used by the early Christians. People in general knew quite well what 'redemption' was. Therefore Christians found it a convenient term to use." Morris then says, "It is our task to try to recapture this meaning and not simply to assume that redemption meant to the ancients what it means to us."[3]

"The Son of Man came to give His life a ransom for many." What was Jesus thinking when He used this term to describe what would be happening in His death?

Focus on the Greek word, *lutron*, translated "ransom." It is derived from the verb *luo*, which simply means "to loose." Morris notes that "it was used of all kinds of loosening; for example, for the loosening of one's clothing, the loosening of

---

2. Leon Morris, *The Apostolic Preaching of the Cross* (London: The Tyndale Press, 1965), 11.
3. Ibid.

armor, of tied animals, and so on."[4] But it was especially used of loosening people from captivity of one sort or another and doing so by payment.

When first-century Greek speakers (and most people in Palestine were) heard the word "redeem" they would have immediately thought in terms of prisoners of war or of slaves being set free or loosed (that is "*luo*-ed") by a payment called the *lutron*, the ransom, the redemption price. Historians have actual documents of the period which used this word.

> So-and-so,
> to the agoranomus, greetings.
> Grant freedom to X, a slave.
>
> She is being set free by ransom *(epi Iutron)*
> by, so-and-so.
> The price paid is 10 drachmae of silver coin and 10 talents,
> 3,000 drachmae of copper. Farewell.[5]

The redemption vocabulary of the Bible is the redemption vocabulary of the marketplace and prisoner of war camp. It is the language of slave auctioneers and hostage negotiators. It has the precise meaning: "release from captivity by payment of a price."

When the Hebrew Old Testament was translated into Greek, it is this "secular" language which is used to convey the intent of Israel's laws. For example, the law stipulated that the first-born human son belonged to the Lord. But the first-born could be bought, actually bought back, for a price. Thus Exodus 13:13: "But every first-born of a donkey you shall redeem with a lamb..." *lutreo.* So too Numbers 18:15-16. Speaking to the priests, Moses says, "Every first issue of the womb of all flesh, whatever man or animal, which they offer to the Lord, shall be yours; nevertheless

---

4.   Ibid., 12.
5.   See Morris, p. 13-14, for more examples.

the first-born of man you shall surely redeem, and the first-born of unclean animals you shall redeem." Another Old Testament example: If a notoriously dangerous bull gored a person to death the bull's owner was to be put to death, unless he redeemed his life by the payment of a price. Exodus 21:30: "If a ransom is demanded of him, then he shall give for the redemption of his life whatever is demanded of him."

One further example: A poor Israelite who had been compelled by economic adversity to sell himself into slavery could be redeemed from slavery either by payment from a relative or by saving up his earnings and paying the price *(lutron)* himself. (Leviticus 25:47-55).

So, what we need to keep in mind is that when first-century Greeks or Hebrews heard the words, "ransom," "redeem" and "redemption," they immediately thought of someone paying a price necessary to free property from mortgage, animals from slaughter, and persons from slavery, even death.[6] And it is this language, with its precise meaning, which Jesus uses when on the road to Jerusalem He says, "The Son of Man came not to be served, but to serve and to give His life as a ransom for many" (Mark 10:45).

It is finished!" was His cry from the cross. What is finished? The ransom!

On the cross, Jesus the Son of God, the Word-made-flesh, the Creator-become-human, Immanuel, God-with-us, paid the price that sets us free! Nothing else needs to be done. The ransom has been paid.

And that is why the cross immediately resonated with the first-century world—a world in which the majority of people

---

6.    John Stott, *The Cross of Christ* (Downers Grove, Ill.: InterVarsity Press, 1986), 176-177.

were slaves, a world in which jails were filled with captured prisoners, a world in which people were overcome with debt. "The Son of Man has come to give His life a ransom" immediately grabbed the imagination of first-century people.

And does it not grab the attention of people in our century? Is not a growing mark of our time "bondage"? Is not the great struggle of our time "addiction"? The cross cries out, "He gives His life a ransom to set the captives free!"

Now, as often happens when vocabulary from one realm of life is employed in another, the ransom-freedom vocabulary soon became "over elaborated."[7] Believers in the second and third centuries began to press the metaphor too far, going beyond Jesus' own use of it. Specifically, people began to ask a question never posed by the New Testament: "*To whom* did Jesus pay the ransom?" Some suggested that Jesus paid it to Satan. And went on to develop strange theories of how the transaction took place, how Satan had been tricked, and so forth. Some suggested that Jesus paid the ransom to God. It was thinkers like Gregory of Nazianus who put a stop to the exaggerated speculations. "Was the ransom paid to the evil one?" he asked. "Monstrous thought! What an outrage, for then the robber receives a ransom." And to the idea that Jesus paid the ransom to the Father, Gregory asks, "How could God delight in the blood of His Son?"[8]

What, then, can we clearly proclaim today in light of Jesus' ransom saying? Six truths gathered around six words: Release, exchange, voluntary, costly, worth, ownership.

---

7. Ibid., 61.
8. Ibid., 62.

# (1) RELEASE. WE ARE RELEASED FROM CAPTIVITY.

In using the word "ransom" Jesus reveals His understanding of the human predicament. He looks at us and sees that we are in bondage from which we cannot free ourselves. And we all know it. Every religious and philosophical system and teacher affirms the fact of human bondage. Something has got a hold on the human species. But most religious and philosophical systems and teachers disagree with Jesus and argue that we can free ourselves from the captivity. That is because they understand the nature of the bondage differently than Jesus does. Some think the bondage is due to ignorance and look to education to redeem us. Some think the bondage is due to totalitarian rule and look to revolutions to redeem us. Some think the bondage is due to our creatureliness and look to new-age techniques to redeem us from our limitations. But for Jesus, the bondage is much deeper and wider and more insidious.

Behind the chains of ignorance and political oppression and creatureliness are chains too strong for us to break. From Jesus' perspective we humans are caught in a complex web; we are slaves to an intricate network of imprisoning masters. The network includes law (Romans 7:3-6; 8:3), sin (Romans 6:18-22; John 8:31-36), unseen spiritual forces (Matthew 12:22; Ephesians 6:12), vanity (1 Peter 1:18-19), and death (Romans 6:20-23; 8:21). There is no way we can free ourselves from those captors. We do not have what it takes. The bondage is so total.

Here is the Good news of the cross! The Son of Man comes into the world and enters into the complex web. And from within, breaks its grip and sets us free. He does not abolish or destroy the captors, yet(!). But He does liberate us from their claim and power. Jesus the ransom-payer releases us from the curse of law, the compulsion of sin, the lordship of unseen powers, the illusion of vain custom and the fear of death.[9]

He really does release us. And he does this now. What has to happen in order for us to go free has happened. "It is finished." The ransom is paid. Nothing else needs to be done. As Jesus says, "If the Son sets you free, you are free indeed" (John 8:36). On the cross Jesus has done what needs to be done to set us free.

This means I can look guilt in the face and say, "You are not my master any more!" I can look sinful habits in the face and say, "You are not my master any more. Jesus releases me from you." I can look evil in the face and say, "You are not my master, be gone in Jesus' name."

Why then do we not walk in greater freedom? Partly because we do not yet fully embrace this Gospel of redemption. Partly because we keep choosing captivity; sometimes secretly enjoying it. And partly because we have not yet taken sin and evil seriously enough. Their grip and power have been broken. But they still hang around. And we keep giving them fresh footholds. Yet, at the cross Jesus has done what needs to be done in order for us to walk free.

How does this happen? The question leads to the second truth offered in Jesus' ransom saying.

## (2) EXCHANGE. HE FREES US FROM BONDAGE THROUGH EXCHANGE.

"The Son of Man came to give His life a ransom for many." Note the word, "for." The Greek word *(anti)* means "in the place of" or "instead of." Jesus comes into the world, enters the prison cell, and

---

9.    J. Blunck, "Freedom," *Dictionary of New Testament Theology.* Vol. 1. (Grand Rapids: Zondervan, 1967), p. 718.

gives His life in place of ours, instead of ours. He exchanges life for life: His life for our life.

The picture the word creates is that of a slave market, full of human beings bought and sold. You are standing, rope around your neck, on the auction block. The auctioneer is taking bids for you. "$100." "$150." "$200." Jesus comes forward and offers, not money, but His own Self, His very life. "I exchange My Self for this one." Exchange. This leads to the third truth affirmed in Jesus' ransom saying.

## (3) VOLUNTARY. HE MAKES THE EXCHANGE — THE GREATEST EXCHANGE OF ALL — VOLUNTARILY.

"The Son of Man gave His life." Not *lost* it, but *gave* it as an act of will, freely chosen. The ransom price is not wrested from Him. Later in Jerusalem Jesus says, "I am the Good Shepherd; the Good Shepherd lays down His life for the sheep . . . no one takes it from Me, but I lay it down on My own initiative" (John 10:11, 18). Jesus pays the ransom voluntarily.

When we read through the record of the last week of Jesus' earthly life, we see that He is not a helpless victim. He is the chief actor in the drama. He is in control. He is choosing the cross. Yes, Judas hands Jesus over to the authorities. Yes, the religious authorities do everything they can to destroy Jesus. Yes, Pilate will not risk his job and do the right thing by releasing Jesus. Yes, the mob is stirred up to shout, "Give us Barabbas . . . Crucify Jesus." But no one is taking Jesus' life from Him. Jesus is giving Himself away. Isn't it ironic that the one who Pilate would not release is the one who releases us? The apostle Paul would later say, in Galatians 2:20, "The Son of God loved me and handed Himself over for me." Jesus makes the exchange that frees, voluntarily. And this makes the fourth truth in Jesus' ransom saying all the more amazing.

## (4) COSTLY. THE VOLUNTARY EXCHANGE WAS VERY COSTLY.

"The Son of Man came to give His life as a ransom for many." His life. His very Self. All that He is. Can you imagine a higher price to pay?

It first of all involved the costliness of the incarnation. "The Son of Man *came*"—this implies "*from* somewhere else" and "*from* another time." The Son of Man who is the Son of God came out of pure Divinity, and became a real flesh-and-blood human. That is, He became what He was not. God the Son became what He was not, which means, God changed the mode of His Being; God changed the constitution of His Being. God the Son became human. For how long? For 33 years? No! Forever! When He rose from the grave He did so bodily. Yes, in a transformed body, but a body nonetheless. He exists with His Father in bodily form, fully God and fully human forever. He became what He was not, forever. What a price to pay.

As I used to say during the Christmas seasons we lived in Manila, I would be willing to become a Filipino, forever, if doing so would make Filipinos free. It would involve all kinds of changes, some costly. But I would be willing to pay the price, for I would still be human. But I would never be willing to become a lizard to set lizards free; or to become a cat to set cats free. To do so would mean becoming, at the most fundamental level, what I am not. God the Son paid the highest price imaginable. God became a human to set men and women free, forever altering the mode of His being.

Actually, the price is higher still. For as a human Jesus the Son then further becomes what He was not: He becomes sin. 2 Corinthians 5:21: "God made Him who knew no sin to be sin on our behalf." It is overwhelming to contemplate what that means. He who knew no sin became Sin. At the cross He became all that we mean by sin; He became filth and greed and lust. We say: "Oh, Lord, no, don't go that far . . . it's not right." His response: "I have to, there is no other way."

And then in His forever-altered mode of Being, and as sin, He gives Himself on the cross. He sheds His blood. He gives it all away. So the apostle Peter can say, "For you know that it was not with perishable things such as silver or gold that you were redeemed from the empty way of life . . . but with the precious blood of Christ (1 Peter 1:18-19). No one has ever paid as high a ransom as Jesus paid.

Why did He do it? The question leads us to the fifth truth being affirmed in Jesus' ransom saying.

## (5) WORTH. JESUS THINKS WE ARE WORTH THE PRICE!

Jesus thinks the captives are worth the price! "Oh Lord, what love is this . . . that pays so dearly?" The Son of Man thinks you and I are worth the ransom price.

I once read the following story; I wish I could remember where. Picture a man dressed in a brand-new suit, wearing a beautiful silk tie, an expensive Swiss watch and a $500 pair of shoes walking along the edge of a sewage pond. As he comes to the place where the sewage is especially thick and gross he stops for a long time and stares into the filth. And then, still dressed in all his elegance, he dives headfirst into the pond. Why? A couple of minutes later he emerges through the garbage and climbs back on the edge of the pond. "Why did you do it?" we ask him. He answers, "To get the diamond that fell in here last week. I'd do anything to get it out."

"The Son of Man came to give His life a ransom for many." Bestowing great dignity upon many, Jesus Christ thinks I am worth His becoming what He was not. I am worth Him becoming my filthy sin. I am worth giving Himself to free me from my filth. And so are you. And so is every other captive crying out for release. This leads us to the sixth truth affirmed in Jesus' ransom saying.

## (6) OWNERSHIP. WE ARE NOW HIS.

What Jesus redeems He owns. That is the only logical conclusion of the ransom vocabulary. The person who pays the ransom has ownership rights over the ones for whom He pays. Jesus has ownership rights over whomever He purchases. He redeems us from captivity in order to make us His own.

"Worthy is the Lamb," sings the redeemed community in the vision recorded in Revelation 5. "Worthy is the Lamb." Why? They sing on, "Because You were slain, and with Your blood purchased men and women for God from every tribe and language and people and nation" (5:9). So the apostle Paul can say to the Corinthians,

> Do you not know that your body is a temple of the Holy Spirit who is in you, whom you have from God, and that you are not your own. For you have been bought with a price; therefore, glorify God in your body (1 Corinthians 6:19-20).

Not your own, bought with a price. That is a powerful basis for holy living. This body is not my own. It is His now. He bought it.

What Jesus redeems He owns. What He pays the price for is His. He frees us from captivity to sin, evil, vanity, and death, for captivity to Him and His extraordinary love.

The fact is we were His before we fell into the filthy web of the prison masters. He gave His life in exchange for ours in order to buy us back. And now we are His forever. In the words of the *Heidelberg Catechism*, "I belong not to myself, but to Jesus Christ, who at the cost of His own blood . . ."

E. Stanley Jones, the missionary to India, whom I count as a mentor, tells a story that pulls it all together for me.[10]

A young boy built a sailboat. He spent days carving the wood, and cutting and sewing cloth for the sails. One day he took the boat to Central Park in New York to test it out on the lake. Having tied a string to the hull, the boy put the boat in the water and gave it a push. All of a sudden a gust of wind caught the sail, more than the boy had bargained for. He let go of the string and the boat was blown out into the middle of the lake. He ran as fast as he could around the lake to catch the boat on the other side. But before he could get there some bullies pulled it out of the water and ran away. Saddened, the young boy started home. Along the way he happened by a pawn shop. And noticed the owner placing the boat in the window. The bullies had already pawned it. The boy ran into the store yelling, "That boat in the window is mine. To which the owner replied, "Sorry kid. I hear lots of sad stories. But it can be yours if you pay for it. The price is $5. The young boy quickly ran home, gathered all his money and ran back to the pawn shop. He went in and gave the owner the $5, and with great joy clutched the boat. As he walked out of the store he was heard to say: "Little boat, you are mine now for two reasons. I made you and I bought you."

"The Son of Man came to give His life a ransom for many."

---

10. He told this in the Philippines while my friend Earl Palmer was pastor of Union Church of Manila; I learned it from Earl. It is a true story.

That is why the cross tugs at the human soul the way it does. That explains its almost magnetic power. At the cross Jesus Christ says to you and to me and to every other person who comes within its orb: "You are mine for two reasons: I made you and now I have bought you."

CHAPTER THREE

# NO MORE SEPARATION

*Matthew 27:45-54*

W e call it "Good Friday." Good? Had we been there that day, as Jesus hung in inconceivably excruciating pain, would we have used the word "good"? Violent Friday. Agonizing Friday. Terrifying Friday. But "Good"? How can anyone use the word "good" to speak of that day?

Let Matthew, the tax-collector turned evangelist, tell us about those three hours.

> Now from the sixth hour darkness fell upon all the land until the ninth hour. And about the ninth hour Jesus cried out with a loud voice, saying, *"Eli, Eli, Lama Sabachthani?"* that is, "My God, My God, why has Thou forsaken me?" And some of those who were standing there, when they heard it, began saying, "This man is calling for Elijah." And immediately one of them ran, and taking a sponge, he filled it with sour wine, and put it on a reed, and gave Him a drink. But the rest of them said, "Let us see whether Elijah will come to save Him." Jesus cried out

again with a loud voice, and yielded up His spirit. And behold, the veil of the temple was torn in two from top to bottom, and the earth shook; and the rocks were split, the tombs were opened; and many bodies of the saints who had fallen asleep were raised; coming out of the tombs after His resurrection they entered the holy city and appeared to many. Now the centurion, and those who were with him keeping guard over Jesus, when they saw the earthquake and the things that were happening, became very frightened and said, "Truly this was the Son of God!" (Matthew 27:45-54)

The words of the text are easy enough to understand: there are no fancy theological terms; we need not appeal to any nuances in the Greek. Yet, as easy as the words are to understand, the mystery they speak goes beyond my ability to grasp. Each time I work in this text I begin to feel like Moses did before the burning bush: I soon feel I ought to take off my shoes. For this text draws us onto holy ground.

What does it all mean?

Darkness at midday for 3 hours.

The earth shaking; rocks splitting without being struck.

Graves breaking open and corpses coming to life.

The curtain in the Temple, that huge, thick curtain in the sanctuary built by Herod the Great, being torn in two from top to bottom.

Phenomena as historical as filling a sponge with wine vinegar and putting it on a stick. What is going on?

I submit to you that it is all directly related to Jesus' cry from the cross: *"Eloi, Eloi, lama sabachthani?"* (27:46). The extraordinary phenomena Matthew describes either interprets or results from this cry, "My God, My God, why hast Thou forsaken Me?"

Given who He is, given the identity of the One who cries, ought there not be some effect in the surrounding environment? The Roman centurion keeping guard at the cross watches Jesus die, witnesses the extraordinary phenomena and realizes that Jesus is no ordinary man. "Surely," he says, "this was the Son of God" (27:54). We do not know what the soldier meant by the title. We do, however, know how Matthew wants us to take it. For Matthew, "Son of God" means "God the Son" (see 11:27). For Matthew, "Son of God" means "Immanuel," "God-with-us" (see 1:18).

If Immanuel cries out from the cross, ought not the cry in some way affect the surrounding environment? If it is "God-with-us" who agonizes so deeply, ought not the created order "feel" the agony?

When He was born into the world through the Virgin Mary the Gospel writers tell us that the darkness of the midnight sky was lit up by the heavenly choir singing for joy. Matthew goes further and tells us that one of the stars in the sky moved. "Look!" he writes, "the star which the magi had seen in the east went on before them, until it came and stood over where the Child was" (see 2:19). The star seems to have been pulled in by the infant Immanuel. If His being born disturbed the natural order, how much more His dying!

Thus can Isaac Watts sings:

> Well might the sun in darkness hide,
> And shut his glories in,
> When God, the Mighty Maker died
> For men the creature's sin[1]

Darkness at midday for three hours. And behold! Look!
The earth shook, the rocks split.
Graves were opened.
And the curtain in the temple was torn from top to bottom.

---

1. "Alas! And Did My Saviour Bleed?", 1707.

All directly related to that *cry* coming from the deepest recesses of Immanuel.

The question, therefore, is what does His cry mean? "My God, My God, why have You forsaken Me?"

Forsaken.

Was He forsaken? It is a strong word; it means "abandoned, cut off, deserted." Was He? Was Jesus of Nazareth, in that moment, objectively forsaken by the One who sent Him? By the One by whom and for whom He lived? Was the Son of God, God the Son, objectively forsaken by God the Father? Or was He only *feeling* forsaken, His feelings having no basis in reality?

However we answer those questions, this story tells us that at minimum Jesus knows the experience of abandonment. Of all human experiences, feeling abandoned by someone you love is the closest to the experience of death. This text shows us that Jesus knows that feeling firsthand. As Dale Bruner says, commenting on this text, Jesus dies before He died.[2] Before His literal death Jesus suffers the death of feeling abandoned. "My God, My God, why have You forsaken Me?" *Why have You forsaken Me? You, My Father, with whom I have lived in intimacy from all eternity? Me, Your only begotten Son, Your greatest delight from all eternity? Why have You forsaken Me?*

Was Jesus actually forsaken? Many interpreters take the position that Jesus was not objectively forsaken, that He was only feeling forsaken. And I can appreciate why they take this position, for the thought that Jesus was really abandoned by God touches the great fear that we could be abandoned by God. If the Father abandons the Son, if God the Father forsakes God the Son, what security do we have?

---

2. Dale Bruner, *Matthew: A Commentary.* Vol. 2 (Dallas: Word, 1990), 1051.

A number of interpreters who take the position that Jesus' "cry of desolation" is not based in reality, argue that, in actual fact, Jesus' cry turns out to be His affirmation that everything is going to be okay. Why? Because the cry, "My God, My God, why have You forsaken Me?" is the first verse of Psalm 22. And, it is argued, that in line with normal Jewish practice, simply by praying the first verse, Jesus is referring to the whole of Psalm 22. And since Psalm 22, although beginning with the raw and frightening feeling of abandonment, ends up with the assurance that everything will be okay, it is argued that this assurance is what Jesus is really resting on in his cry of desolation.

When we read Psalm 22 we are struck by how closely the psalmist's experience parallels Jesus' experience. You would think the psalmist had written Psalm 22 watching the Good Friday events.

> 22:1: "My God, My God, why have You forsaken Me?"
>
> 22:7: "All who see me sneer at me; they separate with the lip, they wag the head saying, 'Commit yourself to the Lord; let Him deliver you; let Him rescue him, because He delights in him'."

This sounds like Matthew 27:41-42: "In the same way the chief priests also, along with the scribes and elders, were mocking Him, saying, 'He saved others; can He not save Himself?" Matthew then quotes Psalm 22:8, "Let Him rescue him." 22:18: "They divide my garments among them, and for my clothing they cast lots." This sounds like Matthew 27:35, about the soldiers at the cross doing just that. And then comes Psalm 22:24: "For He (God) has not despised nor abhorred the affliction of the afflicted; Neither has He hidden His face from them; but when he cried to Him for help, He heard." It is argued then that in citing Psalm 22:1 Jesus is also, and ultimately, citing

43

Psalm 22:24, and is, therefore, affirming that everything will be okay.

I appreciate this line of reasoning.

But I ask, if Jesus in that moment of agony was really saying, that in spite of the agony, He was not forsaken, could He not have prayed a Psalm which says this more clearly? Could He not have prayed the first verse of the Psalm before Psalm 22? "O Lord, in Your strength the King will be glad, And in Your victory how greatly he will rejoice! You have given him his heart's desire . . . " (Psalm 21:1:).

Or better yet, could Jesus not have prayed the first verse of the Psalm after Psalm 22? "The Lord is my shepherd, I shall not want," which leads up to the most perfect line to cite: "Even though I walk through the valley of the shadow of death, I fear no evil, for You are with me" (Psalm 23:4).

But He did not pray that verse because Jesus' feelings of forsakenness had a basis in reality. I agree with New Testament scholar William Lane when he says, "The sharp edge of this word must not be blunted."[3]

Jesus had told His disciples again and again that He must go to Jerusalem and be crucified. Must. Why? To deal with the problem created by human sin and the character of God. Sin separates us from the Living God. Mark the word: separates. Sin cuts us off from the Living God. As Isaiah put it:

> The Lord's hand is not so short that it cannot save;
> Neither is His ear so dull that it cannot hear.
> But your iniquities have made a separation between you and
>     your God,

---

3. William Lane, *The Gospel According to Mark: the English Text with Introduction, Exposition and Notes* (London: Marshall, Morgan & Scott, 1974), 572.

And your sins have hidden His face from you, so that He does
not hear (59:1-2).

Isaiah himself feels this "separation" when in the vision of
the Lord "high and lifted up" he automatically cries out, "Woe is me
. . . for I am an unclean man and dwell among a people of unclean
lips" (6:1-5). Sin separates at a profoundly fundamental level.

Here is the Gospel. At His baptism, in accordance with the
will of His Father, the Son of God chooses to identify with
sinful humanity. The Sinless One became sinful humanity. As
the apostle Paul so boldly puts it, "God made Him who knew no
sin to be sin for us" (2 Corinthians 5:21). And then, at the cross,
again in accordance with the will of His Father, the Son of God
chooses to bear the judgment of God upon human sin.

And what is the nature of that judgment? Is it not separation
from God? Is not the just penalty of sin total alienation from
God? Being cut off from the source of all life?

While hanging on the cross Jesus bore the judgment for
human sin. That is, He bore for us the inevitable separation
which sin causes and deserves. The passion in Jesus' cry matches
the reality of the moment: He is forsaken. In that moment He
is objectively experiencing, as William Lane expresses it, "the
profound horror of separation from God . . . the cry of dereliction
expressed the unfathomable pain of real abandonment by the
Father."[4] *"Eloi, Eloi, lama sabachthani?"*

But how can it be? How can Immanuel, God-with-us, be
abandoned by God? Martin Luther asks, "God forsaken of God,
who can understand it?" That a human being could be forsaken
by God, we shudder to contemplate, but can comprehend. But

---

4.   Ibid., 573.

that the Man from Galilee, the God-man, could be forsaken by God, how can it be? How can there be a real abandonment, a real separation? The Father is God; the Son is God; can God be separated from God?

As incomprehensible as it is, in that moment the inconceivable happens. How can I say it? The real separation from God which we sinners deserve has been taken up by God into God. The total alienation which sin causes is taken up by God to be experienced within God as separation between the Father and the Son. *"Eloi, Eloi. . . ."* I cannot even repeat the rest of the cry.

There is no more mysterious moment in history. There is no more central or pivotal moment in history.

Thus the darkness. And the earth shaking. And the rocks splitting. And the graves opening. And the curtain being torn in two from top to bottom.

*Darkness.* What natural process can account for those three hours of mid-day darkness? I know of none. It could not have been an eclipse, for the moon was full, as it always is at Passover. The darkness had to be God's doing. Throughout Scripture darkness is the sign of judgment. "Darkness over the land" was one of the ten plagues which came upon Egypt when Pharaoh would not let God's people go. Darkness was the token that the land was under a curse.[5] Throughout Scripture darkness is also the sign of separation, the sign of abandonment. So Jesus speaks of hell as the "outer darkness" (Matthew 22:13). The prophet Amos foretold that on the great Day of the Lord darkness would come: "'And it will come about in that day', declares the Lord, 'that I will make the sun go down at noon and make the earth dark in broad daylight. And I will make it like a time of mourning for an only son. . .'"

---

5. See Exodus 10:21ff.

46

(8:9-10). A time of mourning for an only son. Is not the darkness of that Friday not only the judgment of God but the mourning of the Father whose only Son bears the judgment?

*"And the earth shook."* Of course! If He is the Son of God, God the Son, Immanuel, God-with-us, ought not the earth which He sustains by His word tremble as He trembles? Here is "the Ground of our Being," suffering and dying. Ought there not be some sort of cosmic vibration; ought not the created order, at least that part of it closest to the cross, resonate with the pain of its Creator?

*"And the rocks split."* Without being struck. Of course! If the Rock of Ages is splitting inside, ought not the agony send shock waves throughout the universe? When Jesus came into Jerusalem on Palm Sunday the crowds broke out in jubilant praise. The authorities scolded Jesus, telling Him to silence the praise. Jesus said, "If these be silent, the rocks will cry out." On Calvary are not the rocks crying out? Ought not the stones closest to the cross "feel" the impact of what God was experiencing?

*"And the tombs broke open."* Without any human action. And corpses came to life! Here we see the victory of the cross.[6] The Son of God overcomes death through death. Here is what C. S. Lewis, in *The Lion, the Witch and the Wardrobe,* called "the deeper magic"[7]—that by willingly submitting Himself to death Jesus Christ robs death of its finality. At the moment He died, death lost its grip and could no longer hold its captives.

---

6. Which is the subject of the next chapter.
7. For a helpful exposition of Lewis' Christian thought see John P. Bowen, *The Spirituality of Narnia: The Deeper Magic of C. S. Lewis* (Vancouver, B.C.: Regent College Publishing, 2007).

*"And the curtain in the temple was torn in two from top to bottom."* This is the greatest wonder! Matthew is referring to the curtain which separates—mark that word, separates—*separates*—the Holy One from unholy sinners. The curtain separates the rest of the Temple from the Holy of Holies.

Recall that the Jewish temple was made up of a series of rooms.

The first room is called the Court of the Gentiles. For that was as far in as the non-Jews could go.

The second room is called the Court of the Women. For that was as far in as Jewish women could go.

The third room is called the Holy Place. Men could get in there, but even then, there were times when only the priests were allowed.

The fourth room is called the Holy of Holies. Only one man, the High Priest, could go in there, and only once a year on Yom Kippur, the Day of Atonement. And he could only enter after going through an elaborate process of purification. Even then he entered the Holy of Holies, went behind the curtain, at great risk to his life—fearing that if he did not do things correctly, the Holiness of the Place would burn him.

We are told that a rope was tied to the High Priest so that should he die in the Holy of Holies, the other priests could retrieve his body. The curtain was there to separate, separate, separate.

"Behold," says Matthew. Look! The curtain in the temple was torn in two from top to bottom! What did the priests think who were in the temple? There they were, just outside that Holiest of Rooms, offering up the sacrificial Passover Lamb. The whole scene takes place, consciously so, before that huge curtain. The curtain is 60 feet high, 30 feet wide, and nearly 12 inches thick. The priests had no doubt seen the darkness descend. Had they felt the earth shake? And then, mysteriously, that huge curtain rips open, from top to bottom. Did they immediately bow? Did they run for fear of their lives?

Obviously it is an act of God. No one could tear something that thick.

What does it all mean?

It means that the separation between the Holy One and sinners is gone! In that act God is making visible the invisible reality taking place outside the temple up on the hill. The separation has been overcome! There is no longer any need for the curtain. As the Son of God overcomes death through death, so He removes the judgment of forsakenness by suffering the forsakenness Himself. He endured forsakenness so we would not!

William Cowper, a highly respected poet of the 18th century, wrote some of the most beautiful hymns in the English language; hymns like "O For a Closer Walk with God," "God Moves in Mysterious Way His Wonders to Perform," and "There is a Fountain Filled with Blood," celebrating the benefits of the finished work of the cross. Cowper, however, never experienced the joy his words produced in others; he lived nearly all his life fighting depression and despondency, for he lived with fear that, because of his ongoing sinfulness, God might one day finally abandon him. The fear was probably rooted in the fact that his mother died when he was six years old. He never received the healing that is offered for such a deep wound and probably transferred that experience of abandonment to his relationship with God. For all his powerful proclamation of the finished work of Jesus, Cowper never overcame the fear that God might forsake him.

But as a testimony to the triumph of the Gospel, someone chiseled on William Cowper's grave the last stanza of a poem by Elizabeth Barrett Browning. It goes like this:

> Yea, once Immanuel's orphan cry
> His universe hath shaken,
> It went up single, echo-less, My God am I forsaken.
> It went up, from the holy lips, amid the lost creation,
> That of the lost no son should use those words of desolation.

At the cross God suffers the abandonment so we never do! The cry from the darkness that shook the earth, split the rocks, opened the graves, tore the huge curtain has become the declaration: "It is safe to enter the Holy One's Presence. Come, just as you are. Everything that needs to be done has been done. Forsakenness, alienation, abandonment are finished. Come!"

Cheap grace? Not at all. It cost God the incarnation; changing the structure of God's Being forever; God the Son forever taking up our humanity. And it cost God incomprehensible suffering within. And it costs whoever comes, for no one enters the Holy One's Presence without being changed. "For He is like a refiner's fire," says the prophet Malachi. "He will purify the sons of Levi and refine them like gold and silver, so that they may present to the Lord offerings in righteousness" (3:24).

The way in is open, just come. Just as we are? Really? Yes! Shouldn't we first get our act together? No! Besides, which of us can? Which of us, by even our own best effort, can even come close? The curtain can never be torn from the bottom to the top. There is nothing we can do to gain access to the Holy Place.

Ritualism will not do it.

Moralism will not do it.[8]

---

8. As E. Stanley Jones often said.

Mastering right doctrine will not do it.

Adopting the right lifestyle will not do it.

Not that rituals or morals or doctrines or lifestyles do not matter. They do. It is just that none of them overcomes the separation. None of them opens the curtain. None of them opens graves.

"About the ninth hour Jesus cried out in a loud voice, 'Eloi, Eloi, lama sabachthani?' . . . And when Jesus had cried out again in a loud voice, He gave up His Spirit. And look! The curtain in the Temple was torn in two, from top to bottom."

Brothers and sisters: The separation is gone! The separation is gone! No matter which direction you turn, there is no separation.

> In front of you, no separation.
> Behind you, no separation.
> On your right, no separation.
> On your left, no separation.
> Above you, no separation.

Richard Foster is right, when in his book on prayer he says over and over again, "The Father's heart is open wide and you are welcome to come in!" No more separation. The way in is open. Come, just as you are. There is nothing to fear.

Oh yes, the Holy One is still "a consuming fire" (Hebrews 12:29). But in light of the cross we can be sure that the Fire does not consume us; it only consumes that which keeps us from being who God wants us to be.

The separation is gone! Everything that needs to be done to live in intimacy with the Holy One has been done!

And that is why we call it "Good Friday."

CHAPTER FOUR

# GOD'S VICTORY OVER THE POWERS

*Colossians 2:13-15; Hebrews 2:14-15*

When the Portuguese traders first settled in Macau, they built a massive cathedral on the hill overlooking the harbor. But early in the 19th century, one of the violent typhoons that whipped through that part of the world proved too severe and the great cathedral was leveled, all except the front wall. High on top of that wall, "clean cut against the sky,"[1] defying rain, lightning and wind is a great bronze cross. In 1825, when then-governor of Hong Kong, Sir John Bowring, visited Macau he was so moved by the scene that he wrote a hymn which begins, "In the cross of Christ I glory, Towering o'er the wrecks of time."

Powerful phrase, "Towering o'er the wrecks of time." Powerful because it is true.

---

1.  Samuel Zwimer, *The Glory of the Cross* (London: Marshall, Morgan & Scott), 1940, 1.

Why? Why does the cross tower over the wrecks of time? Why has the cross, again and again, defied all assaults against it?

Look at the cross through two texts from two different writers. Listen to the Apostle Paul and to the Christian writer of the letter to the Hebrews.

> And when you were dead in your transgressions and the uncircumcision of your flesh, He made you alive together with Him, having forgiven us all our transgressions, canceled out the certificate of debt consisting of decrees against us and which was hostile to us; and He has taken it out of the way, having nailed it to the cross. When He had disarmed the rulers and authorities, He made a public display of them, having triumphed over them through Him. (Colossians 2:13-15)

> Since then the children share in flesh and blood, He Himself likewise also partook of the same, that through death He might render powerless him who had the power of death, that is, the devil; and might deliver those who through fear of death were subject to slavery all their lives. (Hebrews 2:14-15)

Why does the cross tower over the wrecks of time? Why has the cross, again and again, defied all assaults against it?

At the cross, all the forces that raged against God and God's purposes were overthrown and disarmed. The cross towers over the wrecks of time because the crucified Christ is God's great victory over "the powers". Victory? The cruelty and violence of the crucifixion is a victory? The apparent helplessness and passivity of the cross is a victory?

The Swedish theologian Gustav Aulen argues that this fact is the classic understanding of the achievement of the death of Jesus Christ. By classic he means it was "the ruling idea of the Atonement for the first thousand years of Christian history." For the first thousand years! In his book, *Christus Victor*, Aulen goes to great length to demonstrate that the cross-as-victory-over-the-powers is the dominant New Testament perspective on what happened on Good Friday. "It is finished!" What is finished? At the cross "the principalities and powers" were disarmed. Through death the one who had the power of death was rendered powerless.

Now you may see these words—"at the cross" and "through death—clearly enough. As you have read them, your eyes have seen the words clearly enough: "Cross." "Death." But if you are like the majority of Christians in our time, something went haywire. The phrases your mind heard were *"at the empty tomb"* the principalities and powers were disarmed; *"through the resurrection"* the one who had the power of death was rendered powerless.

That is because most Christians tend to think of the crucifixion as a defeat and the resurrection as the victory. Understandably so: for on that Friday afternoon it appeared that Jesus of Nazareth had been overcome, crushed, destroyed. But that is not the case at all. The crucifixion is the victory! The resurrection is the confirmation of the victory. The resurrection is the celebration of the victory. The resurrection is the beginning of the consequences of the victory. But the victory happened the moment Jesus *died*. The victory took place at the cross through death.

Read through the texts in the New Testament, which speak of overcoming, conquest, triumph, and you will discover that nearly all of them are in the context of the cross, in the context of the death of Jesus. Is this not the point of the grand vision in Revelation 5? John hears one of the elders declare "The Lion has overcome!" (5:5). And John turns around to see not a lion, but a Lamb. And John hears all of creation sing a new song, "Worthy is the Lamb." Why? Why is the Lamb worthy? Because He rose again? Yes. But that is not what is celebrated by the heavenly choir. "Worthy is the Lamb . . . because You were slain" (5:9). Worthy is the Lamb who was slain. Yes, the Lamb rose again and is alive. But the Lamb *overcame* the moment He was slain. The Lamb won the victory through death.

Listen to the texts again, this time from the New International Version of the Bible. Colossians 2:15: "And having *disarmed* the powers and authorities, He (God) made a public spectacle of them, *triumphing* over them *by the cross*."

And Hebrews 2:14: "Since the children have flesh and blood, He too shared in their humanity so that *by His death* He might destroy him who holds the power of death—that is, the devil."

Texts like these call for a paradigm shift in our understanding of reality. Texts like these tell us that there is more going on around us than meets the unaided intellect. There is more to the movement of history and to this particular moment in history than we can discern with our century's eyes and ears.

In the Colossians text Paul refers to "powers and authorities." And as you can imagine there is considerable debate about what Paul means by the terms. Some argue that he is simply referring to human powers and authorities. And as we all know, some human powers and authorities seek and cooperate with the will of God; others do not. Indeed, others seek, as the Psalmist puts it, to "throw off the fetters" of God and God's anointed. (Psalm 2:2). Some human powers and authorities reject the presence and claims of the Living God and usurp the power and authority of God in human life. Clearly, such human powers and authorities, both secular and religious, were involved in the death of Jesus: Caiphas and Pilate, their named representatives.

But it seems that Paul has something more in mind when he uses those terms. Earlier in Colossians, specifically 1:16, he declares that all things were created by Christ: "things in heaven and on earth, visible and invisible, whether thrones or powers or rulers or authorities." Visible and invisible, on earth and in heaven, powers and authorities. It seems he is speaking of supra-human powers and authorities.

The issue is settled for me by how Paul uses the terms in Ephesians, specifically 6:12: "For our struggle is not against flesh and blood, but against the rulers, against the authorities, against the powers of this dark world and against the spiritual forces of evil in the heavenly realms."

These supra-human powers and authorities work in and with and alongside human powers and authorities, more than we care to know. That is the point of the vision recorded for us in Revelation, chapters 12 through 14. There we see a great dragon who tries to kill the Child of the woman. The dragon is the Evil one. The Child is Jesus Christ. Since the dragon cannot, however, overcome the Child, he goes after the friends of the Child, the people of God. But not directly. The dragon mounts his assault through two forces pictured as beasts; one from the sea, representing corrupt and arrogant political systems; the other from the earth, representing deceived and deceiving religious systems.[2]

At the cross God in Christ is doing battle (did battle) with the Dragon and his beasts; at the cross God in Christ is doing battle (did battle) with the Devil and his principalities.

The conflict began long before that Friday. It began that day the first humans believed the serpent's lie—that to live independent from God means freedom and life. In the Garden

---

2. See my *Discipleship on the Edge: An Expository Journey through the Book of Revelation* (Vancouver, BC.: Regent Publishing, 2004) for a fuller treatment of these ideas.

God says to the serpent: "Cursed are you . . . and I will put enmity between you and the woman and between your offspring and hers; he will crush your head and you will strike his heal" (Genesis 3:14-15).

The conflict intensified in the history of Israel.

Then on Christmas Eve the final battle began. King Herod, under the influence of the beast from the earth, sought to destroy the infant Jesus. When Jesus became an adult, the attempt to destroy Him came from the religious establishment under the influence of the beast from the sea. It all came to a head when the powers and authorities—human, yes, but also, and primarily, supra-human—nailed Jesus to the cross. "It is finished."

What is finished?

Colossians 2:15: "And having disarmed the powers and authorities, God made a public spectacle of them, triumphing over them by the cross."

Hebrews 2:14: "He became like us, so that by His death He might destroy him who holds the power of death."

So much more was going on that Friday than anyone present could have imagined!

In the Colossians text Paul uses vivid language. He says that God "disarmed" the powers and authorities. Literally, God stripped them of their weapons and ultimate strength. And Paul says God "made a public display/spectacle" of the powers and authorities, meaning that God revealed their inherent weakness and foolishness, demonstrating that, after all, they are, in the words of Peter O'Brien, "powerless powers."[3] And Paul says God was "triumphing over" the powers and authorities by the cross.

---

3. Peter O'Brien, *Colossians, Philemon* (Milton Keynes, England: Word, 1987), 129.

The language triggers a specific picture. In the words of William Barclay,

> The picture is that of the triumph of a Roman general. When a Roman general had won a really notable victory, he was allowed to march his victorious armies through the streets of Rome and behind him followed the kings and the leaders and the peoples he had vanquished. They were openly branded as his spoils. Paul thinks of Jesus as a conqueror enjoying a kind of cosmic triumph, and in his triumphal procession are the powers of evil, beaten forever, for everyone to see.[4]

And the mystery is this: the triumph takes place at the cross. The Hebrews text puts it most succinctly: "through death He (Christ) destroyed the one who had the power of death."

Again, although the language of the texts is very clear, we tend to transpose it, and in place of "at the cross" we read, "at the empty tomb"; and in place of "through death" we read, "through resurrection." I have done this many times. I have said on many Easter mornings: "On Friday the devil and all his powers unleashed all their evil against Jesus Christ. And it appeared that they had won. And for three days they celebrated, crying, 'We won, we won.'"

But the fact is, they did not celebrate. For in the moment Jesus died, the powers were defeated and they knew it. Knew it? They knew it?

Is this not the point Matthew makes in his telling of the crucifixion events? I have come to trust Matthew as a brilliant theologian. Matthew writes in chapter 27, verses 50-52:

> And when Jesus had cried out again in a loud voice, He gave up His spirit. And behold! And look! The veil in the temple was

---

4. William Barclay, *Letters to the Philippians, Colossians and Thessalonians* (Edinburgh: Saint Andrew Press, 1960), 143.

torn in two from top to bottom. The earth shook and the rocks split. The tombs were opened and the bodies of many holy people who had died were raised to life.

The reference to the veil being torn in two, we can grasp: through the death of Jesus Christ the way into the Holy of Holies has been opened.[5] But what are we to make of the reference to the rocks splitting and the graves being opened? "Jesus gave up His spirit. And the graves were opened."

What is going on here? Should this text not be in the next chapter, *after* Easter? No! Matthew is declaring the power of the cross: The death of the Son of God was the deathblow to Satan's rule of death.[6] In the moment Jesus died, the grip of death was broken; death could no longer hold its prisoners and the graves had to open! Is this not wonderful news?

This helps us understand another difficult text. It is a line in the Apostle Peter's sermon on the Day of Pentecost. Peter says: "God raised Jesus up again, putting an end to the agony of death, since it was impossible for Him to be held in its power" (Acts 2:24). That bothered me because it seems to lean in the direction of docetism—in the direction of the heresy which says the Son of God only *appeared* to become human (but did not really), and only *appeared* to die. "It was impossible for Him to be held in its power." The line seems to say the death of Jesus was not a real death.

But it was a real death. Jesus did die. Peter's point is this: It was impossible for death to hold the dead Jesus because in the death of Jesus, death lost its grip. At the moment Jesus died, death already lost its finality. Death could no longer hold on, even to the dead Jesus. This is why a dear friend of mine, Peter Joshua, now

---

5. So Hebrews 4:14-16; 9:11-12.
6. John Eades, sixteenth-century Scottish commentator.

departed, could say, "When death stung Jesus, it stung itself to death."

Now we can appreciate Jesus' words just before going to the cross. "The hour has come . . . unless a grain of wheat falls into the ground and dies it lives all alone but if it dies it becomes much wheat." (John 12:23-24). "Now judgment is upon the world; now the ruler of this world shall be cast out." (John 12:31). Now? In the weakness of the cross? Yes! The cross is the dethronement of the powers and the enthronement of Jesus Christ.[7]

That is why the cross "towers over the wrecks of time." Christ crucified is the victory of God over the powers. It is a part of God's "foolish" wisdom and "weak" power Paul speaks of in I Corinthians. Through (apparent) defeat God wins the victory.

Thus Paul says in 1 Corinthians 2:8: If the rulers of this age had understood God's "foolish" wisdom "they would not have crucified the Lord of glory." Paul is not saying that if the powers had known who Jesus really was they would not have crucified Him. The fact is, they did know who He was. Again and again in the Gospels we hear the powers say: "I know who You are—the Holy One of God!" (Mark 1:24). And they knew why He became a man. "Have You come to destroy us?" What they did not know is the mystery, the wisdom of God; namely, that by crucifying the Lord of Glory they would be defeated.

Let John R.W. Stott summarize this understanding of the cross:

> Of course any contemporary observer, who saw Christ die, would have listened with astonished incredulity to the claim that the crucified was a conqueror. Had he not been rejected by his own nation, betrayed, denied and deserted by his own disciples, and executed by authority from the Roman procura-

---

7.   G.R. Beasley-Murray, *John* (Waco, Texas: Word Books, 1999), 214.

tor? Look at him there, spread-eagle and skewered on his cross, robbed of all freedom of movement, strung up with nails or ropes or both, pinned there and powerless. It appears to be total defeat. If there is victory, it is the victory of pride, prejudice, jealousy, hatred, cowardice and brutality. Yet the Christian claim is that the reality is the opposite of the appearance. What looks like (and indeed was) the defeat of goodness by evil is also, and more certainly, the defeat of evil by goodness. Overcome there, he was himself overcoming. Crushed by the ruthless power of Rome, he was himself crushing the serpent's head (Gen. 3:15). The victim was the victor, and the cross is still the throne from which he rules the world."[8]

The implications of this understanding of Christ's death—of the center of our faith—are staggering. Consider just three.

1. The first implication, in the words of Amy Carmichael, is this: "We live from victory, not toward victory." Although evil still abounds, it has been defeated. The fact is, the more aware the principalities and powers are of this (their) defeat the more ferocious they become, like a dragon in its death throes. Evil governments step up the evil when they know they are losing. Gangs turn up the heat when they know they are losing.

Which means humanity does not have to bow down to or cooperate with the powers. We do this, but *we do not have to*. The powers are still alive, but they are ultimately powerless powers.

The word in Hebrews 2:14 translated as "destroy" literally means "make ineffective or inactive." It is used to describe unproductive land and unfruitful trees.[9] The land and the trees are still there, but they are barren. The powers have not been

---

8. John R.W. Stott, *The Cross of Christ* (Downers Grove, Ill.: InterVarsity Press, 1986), 227-228.

9. Ibid., 240.

"liquidated" but they have been "neutralized." Their weapons have been rendered ineffective.

What are the weapons evil uses to get its way in the world? They are two: accusation and fear. The New Testament speaks of the powers accusing people of sin and holding people in bondage through fear of death. Both weapons have been broken at the cross. Colossians 2:14 declares that God has taken the decree of our indebtedness and wiped it off, nailing it to the cross, canceling all our debts. There are no longer any grounds for accusation. Hebrews 2:14 declares that Death has lost its finality. To be threatened with death will no longer work, for we know that death is not the end.

As Martin Luther wrote in his hymn, *A Mighty Fortress is Our God,*

> Let goods and kindred go,
> This mortal life also
> The body they may kill;
> God's truth abideth still:
> His kingdom is forever.

The conflict goes on. But the decisive battle has been fought and won. We do not wrestle with flesh and blood, but with powers and authorities. And the good news is that we wrestle with defeated powers and authorities. We can look any form of evil in the face and say, "You are a defeated foe, you must bow to the name of Jesus." We work from the victory, not towards it.

2. Second implication: We know how disciples of Jesus are to overcome. How? The same way He did. He overcame by death. And so do we.

> "And they overcame the dragon because of the blood of the Lamb and because of the word of their testimony, and because

63

they did not love their life even to death"—or "they did not love their lives so much as to shrink from death." (Revelation 12:11)

Evil only gains where it is not resisted. It is not resisted because men and women are afraid that if they resist they will die. You have likely seen the poster that says, "All that evil needs is for enough good men to keep silent." Good men keep silent because they want to keep their lives. However, dare to risk the cost of resistance and the stronghold of evil is broken.

This is what we see in all the great human liberation movements of the past century. Study the movement in India when nearly a fifth of the world's population was freed to be themselves. Study the civil rights movement in America in the 1960s, when people held down for decades simply because of the color of their skin were freed to be themselves. Study the movement that took place in the Philippines which culminated in the so-called People Power Revolution of 1986, when Filipinos were freed to be themselves.

Study those movements and you discover one common denominator. Each of those movements was inspired (on the human level) by people who understood the wisdom of God's "weak" ways. Each of those movements was inspired by people who read the New Testament and discovered the mystery. I am referring to people like Mahatma Gandhi in India, Martin Luther King, Jr., in America, Ninoy Aquino in the Philippines, Lech Walesa in Poland, Alexander Dubcek, and Vaclau Havel in Czechoslovakia. Each of them, in very different circumstances read the New Testament and, understanding the victory of the cross, followed Jesus' risky ways.

For me, the most powerful example is Ninoy Aquino because he, more than any other I know, understood the mystery. In the early 1980s he was arrested and put in prison by the dictator Ferdinand Marcos for speaking out against Marcos' oppressive policies. While in prison he read the New Testament and began to see. He also developed a serious heart condition. Through the intermediary, U.S. President Jimmy Carter, Aquino was allowed to leave the Philippines and go to Boston for surgery. While recuperating he read the New Testament and saw even more. Although he could have remained in the safety of the United States, he felt constrained to return to the Philippines, knowing full well that he would probably be killed. He was warned by all kinds of people that this time the Marcos forces would do him in. But he felt he had to go home, inspired by the victory of the cross.

In August of 1982, he left the U.S., flying back home through Taipai, Taiwan. When his plane landed at Manila International Airport soldiers boarded it to escort Ninoy off. Just after passing through the front door of the plane, gunshots rang out. Mr. Aquino fell down the stairs, onto the airport tarmac, dead. A bullet through his head. In his coat pocket were the papers of the speech he was going to give to the waiting press corps. And the opening line of that speech is: "The willing sacrifice of the innocent is the most powerful answer to insolent tyranny that has yet been conceived by God or man."[10]

And through daring to risk his life, he overcame. Overcame? Yes! The killing of Aquino achieved exactly the opposite of what the Marcos forces wanted. It did not silence the cause of freedom. The killing fanned it to flame! Three days after the murder two million Filipinos silently walked through the streets of Manila behind Ninoy's casket. And three years after the murder three million Filipinos poured into the freeway outside the military headquarters saying, without guns or rocks, *"Tapas na,"* "enough is enough."

---

10. See Charles Colson with Ellen Santilli Vaughn, *Kingdoms in Conflict* (New York: William Morrow, 1989).

As I said many times to people in Manila in the days after the People Power Revolution: "Never forget, the victory was won on the airport tarmac. It was manifested three years later on the freeway. But the victory was won on the tarmac, the moment they killed Aquino." There is, in the part of Manila where we lived, a statue of Ninoy falling down a set of stairs and a dove alighting from his shoulders. I drove by the statue often, and 1 Cor. 2:8 regularly came to mind: "If they had known the wisdom of God they would not have crucified the Lord of Glory."

You would think that the principalities and powers would have gotten it by now. Any time any disciple of the Crucified Lord risks and follows the way of the cross, evil is overcome. The risk need not be as dramatic as Aquino. Indeed, what is needed is hundreds and thousands of us ordinary Christians simply resisting by risking rejection, comfort, reputation, promotion. Going the way of the Lamb, risky as it is, always finally overcomes.

3. There is a third implication of "the cross-as-victory." We need not be afraid. The turmoil in the world is heating up again. It often feels to me as though a restraining force, once holding evil in check, has collapsed. We may be in for a very rocky time. But we need not be afraid.

Disciples of Jesus never need feel intimidated by the powers. Disciples of Jesus never need imitate the powers either, which is what we often do when we feel intimidated. When the Church becomes afraid of what is happening in the world and develops a "fortress" mentality, it means the Church has lost touch with the resurrection. But more importantly, it means we have lost touch with the cross.

When the history of the twenieth century is written, the greatest story will be the breaking of the grip of communism in

Eastern Europe and the old Soviet Union. And if the historians "have eyes to see," they will realize that the heroes were disciples of Jesus who, not thinking themselves brave, responded to unspeakable evil in the power of cruciform love, choosing to overcome evil with good.

In his books, *Kingdoms in Conflict* and *The Body*, Charles Colson tells story after story of individuals and congregations facing the evil in light of the cross. Colson traces all the stirrings of the past decades to what was happening in Poland, in a place called Nowa Huta. Nowa Huta, "New Town," was designed by the Communists as a center for workers, who were to make up the backbone of the new Poland. Colson describes this "ideal" town as, "mammoth steel works and ugly chimneys spewing smoke and sulfuric fumes into the sky."[11]

Curiously, when Nowa Huta was built the Communists left an open square in the town center. The workers requested that a church be built. The Communists responded: A church? Why a church? This is the new world. Besides haven't we Communists given you Poles more than you need? Just go back to work.

So several young Christians and a Priest nailed together two rugged beams and pounded the timber cross into the ground where they wanted the church to be. And night after night people gathered around that cross for worship. And night after night the authorities retaliated with water cannons, chasing the people away and tearing down the cross. And morning after morning the cross would reappear. By night, people again gathered for worship. And again, they were chased away. This went on for years: The authorities tearing the cross down, the people putting it back up.

---

11. Charles Colson with Ellen Santilli Vaughn, *The Body* (Dallas: Word 1992), 201.

Colson suggests that the Nowa Huta's struggle symbolized what was happening all over Eastern Europe and Russia. Believers alarmed by the power of evil, but not developing a fortress mentality, moving out in the victory of the cross.

T. S. Elliot captured this spirit in his play, *Murder in the Cathedral*. The great Cathedral of Canterbury was under siege by would-be assassins. Out of understandable fear, the priests barred the door to the Cathedral. But Thomas the Archbishop would not allow it.

"Unbar the doors! Throw open the doors! I will not have the house of prayer, the Church of Christ, the sanctuary, be turned into a fortress. . . the Church shall be opened, even to our enemies. Open the door!"

The priests, thinking Thomas was crazy, protested: "You would bar the door against the lion, the leopard, the wolf or the boar, why not more against beasts with the souls of damned men, against men who would damn themselves to beast."

Thomas answered: "We have fought the beasts and have conquered . . . Now is the triumph of the cross. Now, open the door! I command it. Open the door!"

"In the cross of Christ I glory, towering o'er the wrecks of time" because in the cross of Christ, God won the victory over all the powers which threaten to undo us.

# CHAPTER FIVE

# THE GLORIFICATION
# OF GOD

*John 12:20-25*

We turn now to the Apostle John for help in answering our question: "What is finished?" And we turn to the theological center of his Gospel. Everything that happens *before* flows towards it; everything that happens *after* flows from it. Indeed, in this text we are brought to the theological center of the whole Christian story.

> Now there were some Greeks among those who were going up to worship at the feast; These then came to Philip, who was from Bethsaida of Galilee, and began to ask him, saying, "Sir, we wish to see Jesus." Philip came and told Andrew; Andrew and Philip came and told Jesus. And Jesus answered them, saying, "The hour has come for the Son of Man to be glorified. "Truly, truly, I say to you, unless a grain of wheat falls into the earth and dies, it remains alone; but if it dies, it bears much

fruit. "He who loves his life loses it, and h who hates his life in this world will keep it to life eternal." (John 12:20-25)

*"Sir, we wish to see Jesus."*

The Greeks who had come to Jerusalem to celebrate the Jewish Feast of Passover understandably wanted to see the person about whom the whole city was in an uproar. The Greeks had witnessed the joyous celebration taking place along the highway as Jesus rode into the city on the back of a donkey. And the Greeks had witnessed that intense scene inside the city, when Jesus walked through the temple precincts, fashioned a whip from the straw lying all around and drove out the money changers and sacrifice-animal sellers. The Greeks had heard Jesus say, "My house shall be called a house of prayer for all the nations" (Mark 11:7). The Greeks were moved by the fact that this Jewish Man cared so much about non-Jews having a place to pray that He risked His own life.[1]

*"Sir, we wish to see Jesus."*

They ask Philip, because of all the disciples of Jesus, he had a Greek name. "We wish to see Jesus." They mean more than "we want to get a closer look at the fellow." They mean "we want to meet Him and understand who He is and what makes Him tick."

*"Sir, we wish to see Jesus."*

So do I.

So do you.

Jesus responds to the request in a way that no one—Greek or Jew—expected. No one, that is, except Jesus' Father.

There are four key terms in Jesus' response to that Palm Sunday request. They are: Lifted up, glorify, hour, and grain of wheat.

---

1. Michael Card, *The Parable of Joy: Reflections on the Wisdom of the Book of John* (Nashville: Thomas Nelson Publishers, 1995), 155.

*Lifted up.* First, Jesus says in John 12:32, "If I be *lifted up* I will draw all people to Myself." We know, from the way the expression "lifted up" is used in other places in Jesus' Gospel, that Jesus is speaking of being lifted up onto the cross.

In John 3:14, in the middle of His late-night conversation with Nicodemus, Jesus says, "Just as Moses *lifted up* the snake in the desert so the Son of Man must be *lifted up*, that everyone who believes in Him may have eternal life." Jesus is referring to that event in Israel's history when, after being miraculously freed from bondage in Egypt, the people began to grumble and complain, and spoke out against Moses and God. "Fiery snakes," says the text, were "sent among the people and they bit the people so that many died" (Numbers 21:6). Moses prayed to God, and was told to make a replica of the snakes, put the replica on a pole, and [get] put the pole in the midst of the people. When anyone who had been bitten looked up at the *up-lifted* snake she or he would be healed.

The phrase "if I be lifted up" on Jesus' lips means "if I be attached to a pole and lifted up in the midst of the people." He is speaking of the healing, saving power of His death. "If I be lifted up, I will draw all people to Myself." Note the verb, "I *will draw.*" It is crucial for the church's work in the world. Jesus is telling us that what draws people more than anything else is Him crucified.

Yes, He has been resurrected. And we point people to that great fact! He who died is now alive(!), and can be known. Yes, we point people to His birth, to the mystery of Divinity taking on our humanity, the Creator becoming a Creation. And yes, we point people to His Ascension. And yes, we point people to His coming again. But it is His death, more than anything else, that draws people. Why?

71

This leads to the second key term in Jesus' response to the Greeks.

*Glorify.* Jesus says—verse 23—"the hour has come for the Son of Man to be *glorified.*" "Son of Man" was Jesus' favorite self-designation.

"The hour has come for the Son of Man to be glorified." And for the Father to be glorified. Jesus says in John 12:28, "Father! Glorify your name!"

*Glorify.* What does this verb mean? Two things. Manifest and honor. The "Glory of God" is "the weightiness of God's self-manifestation." To glorify God is to manifest the essential weightiness of God. And having recognized that essential weightiness, to honor it. Manifest and honor. The hour has come for Jesus as the Son of Man to be manifested for who He is. And then be honored. The hour has come for Jesus' Father to be manifested for who He is and then be honored.

"For *this purpose* I have come to this hour," says Jesus (John 12:27). To glorify the Name of God, to manifest and honor the Name of God. "Name" is a way of saying "nature and character." To glorify the name of God is to glorify the nature and character of God. The moment has come for the nature and character of Jesus the Son of Man and God the Father to be manifested and honored.

John tells us that when Jesus cried out, "Father glorify your name!" a voice came from heaven saying, "I have glorified it, and I will glorify it again (12:28). "I have . . . and I will (see also John 13:31-32; 17:4).

"I have." How? In the works of Jesus which He has already done. Works which He says are the works of His Father. In His deeds of mercy and restoration Jesus had already glorified His Father's Name; He had already manifested and honored the Father's nature and character. Turning water into wine and raising Lazarus from the dead, for instance, manifest and honor who the Living God is. The God who cares for us in and as Jesus brings new life out of the old! Indeed, this God brings new life out of death!! "I have glorified it!"

And yet, throughout Jesus' ministry we learn that there is a particular moment yet to come when the Divine Glory will become more clearly evident. More evident than raising Lazarus? Yes! "I *have* glorified it . . . and I *will* glorify my name," says the Father. Which leads us to the third key term in Jesus' response to the Greeks.

*Hour.* Jesus says in John 12:23 "the hour has come." Trace the use of this word "hour" through John's Gospel and [you] we see that it always points to Jesus' death.

John 7:30—"They were seeking therefore to seize Him; and no one laid a hand on Him, because His *hour* had not yet come."

John 8:20—"These words He spoke in the treasury as He taught in the temple; and no one seized Him, because His hour had not yet come."

The "hour" has come for Him to be seized by people who want to destroy Him. On Palm Sunday, just after entering the Holy City to the shouts of "Hosanna," Jesus says, "the hour has come." The not-yet is now. Jesus would reiterate this two more times: Just after Judas leaves the Upper Room (13:30) and while Jesus is praying in the Garden of Gethsemane (17:1).

The hour for violent people to lay their hands on Him; the hour to be seized had come.

Now, put the first three key terms together: Lifted up, glorify, hour. "Sir, we wish to see Jesus." They want to understand who He is, to understand what makes Him tick. Jesus responds, "the

73

hour has come for the Son of Man to be glorified and to glorify the Father, as I be lifted up . . . "

The point of all this? Jesus' death on the cross is the *glorification* of the Name of God! Jesus' death on the cross, His handing Himself over to those who want to destroy Him, is the great moment when the nature and character of the Living God is finally, decisively manifested and honored.

This is why John Calvin spoke of the cross as "the theatre of glory." Calvin wrote:

> For in the cross of Christ, as in a splendid theatre, the incomparable goodness of God is set before the whole. The glory of God shines indeed, in all creation, on high and below, but never more bright than in the cross . . . If it be objected that nothing could be less glorious than Christ's death, I reply that in that death we see a boundless glory.[2]

The death of Jesus—the great moment of glory. This is glory? Yes! It is all part of the scandal of the Gospel, the great reversal of values. The moment of apparent defeat is victory—"Now is the judgment of the world," declares Jesus, "now the ruler of this world will be driven out" (12:31). The moment of apparent humiliation is glory. Jesus is saying to the Greeks, and to the Jews, and to us: "Here in the cross, as nowhere else, the nature and character of the Living God is manifested and honored. Here is glory!"

Michael Green puts it so well in his book, *The Empty Cross of Jesus*. He writes: "Perhaps the greatest paradox in the Gospel, assisted by the ambiguity in the word "lifted up," is the repeated assertion that the lifting up of the Son of Man on the cross is not the precursor to his being raised in glory but actually is His exaltation." Then Green writes this: "It would be hard to make the

---

2. Quoted by John Stott, *The Cross of Christ* (Downers Grove, Ill.: InterVarsity Press, 1986), 206.

point more clearly that the supreme glory of deity is the stoop of Calvary."[3]

No one, however, put it more clearly than Jesus Himself. And this leads us to the fourth key term in Jesus' response to the Greeks on Palm Sunday.

"Grain of Wheat." Jesus says in John 12:24, "Truly, truly (amen, amen)"—which is Jesus' way of saying, 'You can build your life on this'—"I say to you, unless a grain of wheat falls into the ground and dies it remains by itself alone; but if it dies, it bears much fruit."

Of whom is Jesus speaking when He uses the grain of wheat analogy? Of Himself! "The hour has come for the Son of Man to be glorified." "Unless a grain of wheat falls into the ground and dies . . . " "The hour has come . . . Father, glorify your Name!" "Unless a grain of wheat falls into the ground and dies . . . "

The moment has come for the nature and character of Jesus the glorious Son of Man to be decisively manifested and honored; the moment has come for the nature and character of His Father to be decisively manifested and honored; and Jesus speaks of a grain of wheat falling and dying! This is the irony of ironies! (or paradox of all paradoxes).

A grain of wheat only lives if it dies to itself. It fulfills its reason for being as it gives itself away in death. Indeed it if does not die it does not love; it merely exists, alone and unfulfilled.

"Sir, we wish to see Jesus"—to understand what makes him tick. "Truly, truly I say to you, unless a grain of wheat . . . "

The secret of Jesus' identity and therefore the secret of His Father's identity, lies in the self-giving of the grain of wheat!

---

3. Michael Green, *The Empty Cross of Jesus*, 52.

This understanding of Glory is what is celebrated in that early Christian hymn recorded by the apostle Paul in Philippians 2:5-11.

> Let this mind be in you which was also in Christ Jesus, who, though He existed in the form of God, did not consider equality with God something to take advantage of, but emptied Himself, taking the form of a servant, being made in human likeness. And being found in human appearance, He humbled Himself by being obedient to the point of death, even death on a cross. Therefore also God highly exalted Him, and bestowed on Him the name which is above every name, that at the name of Jesus every knee should bow, of those who are in heaven, and on earth, and under the earth, and that every tongue should confess that Jesus Christ is Lord, to the glory of God the Father.

To the glory of God the Father? How does Jesus' descent from the heights to the depths glorify the Father?

The crucial line in the hymn is, "He did not consider equality with God to be . . . but . . ." The language suggests that in His pre-earthly state, Jesus the Son of God is contemplating what it means to be equal with God the Father. And He comes to a conclusion which no one (except the Father!) expects. He concludes that being equal with God is not something to be exploited, not something to take advantage of. Quite the opposite is true. For Jesus, being equal with God means emptying One's Self, giving One's life away.

The Son of God, who has always been equal with the Father, is contemplating what it means to be like the Father, what it means to be God. And He comes to the conclusion that to-be-like-the-Father—that to be God—means to *live* by giving yourself away in servant love.

When, therefore, the Son of God comes to earth and lives the servant life—"unless a grain of wheat"—He is not giving up "the form of God" or "equality with God." How could He? How can

God no longer be God? The answer is that he cannot and he does not. He does not lay aside "the form of God" or "equality with God." He does not "lay aside" His glory. Rather, He lives the servant life because He considers the servant life to be the most appropriate way to manifest and honor what He has seen in the Father from all eternity. He considers that "being in the form of God," and "having equality with God," is most appropriately, most inherently, most essentially expressed in emptying Himself, taking on the form of a servant, accepting the powerlessness and mortality of our humanity, and dying the death of a criminal. "Unless a grain of wheat falls to the ground and dies."

This is how N. T. Wright puts it.

> Nothing described by either "in the form of God" or by "to be equal with God" is given up. Rather it is re-interpreted, understood in a manner in striking contrast to what one might have expected. Over against the standard picture of oriental despots, who understood their position as something to be used for their own advantage, Jesus understood His position to mean self-negation.[4]

Biblical scholar C. F. D. Moule further notes: "Divine equality does not mean "getting" but "giving." It is properly expressed in self-giving love."[5]

In becoming a human being, Jesus the eternal Son of God, did not cease to be what He was; He did not renounce His Divinity; He did not strip Himself of Divinity. It was exactly the opposite: Jesus was expressing what all that Divinity really means! He did not consider equality with God something to use for his own

---

4.   N. T. Wright, "*Harpagmos* and the Meaning of Phil. 2:5-11," *Journal of Theological Studies*, 37 (1986): 321-352.
5.   Ibid.

advantage. Rather, He considered equality with God to be self-emptying servanthood.

The Son of God, who from all eternity possesses the form of God, who from all eternity is equal with God the Father, understands being God in terms of incarnation, servanthood, crucifixion. The Son of God, who from all eternity possesses the form of God, who from all eternity is equal with God the Father, understands being God in terms of cradle, towel, cross. The real humiliation of the incarnation and the cross, writes N. T. Wright,

> . . . is that one who was Himself God, and who never during the whole process stopped being God, could embrace such a vocation. The real theological emphasis of the hymn [Philippians 2:5-11], therefore, is not simply a new view of Jesus. It is a new understanding of God, of Father; a re-definition of Father. Against the age-old attempts of human beings to make God in their own (arrogant, self-glorifying) image, Calvary reveals the truth about what it meant to be God . . . incarnation and even crucifixion are to be seen as appropriate vehicles for the dynamic self-revelation of God."[6]

That is why the hymn sings, "Therefore, God has highly exalted Jesus the Servant." That is why the Crucified One is given the Name above every name, the Name LORD; in Greek, *Kurios;* in Hebrew, Yahweh. God the Father gives the Name Yahweh to Jesus the Son because in the Son's decision to give Himself in self-emptying love, the Son has rightly understood what it means to be Yahweh. It is because He emptied Himself, it is because He took on our humanity, it is because He became a Servant, it is because He laid down His life for us on the cross that He is worthy of the Name LORD, *Kurios,* Yahweh.

---

6. Ibid.

The title is not granted because Jesus is exalted to the throne; the title is granted because He emptied Himself. Self-giving love is the proper expression of Divine Glory. "The passion of Jesus was not His human misfortune; it was the decisive manifestation of His divinity."[7]

In granting Jesus Christ the Name above every name, God the Father "is, as it were, endorsing that interpretation of divine equality which the Son adopted."[8]

"Sir, we wish to see Jesus."

"Unless a grain of wheat falls into the ground and dies...."

They were not easy words to say. Jesus knew full well what it would entail for Him. "Now is my soul *troubled*." The verb conveys shock, agitation, and revulsion. "Now my soul is troubled; and what shall I say, 'Father, save me from this hour? No, it is *for this purpose* I have come to this hour. Father! Glorify Your Name" (12:27-28)!

That is the deepest passion of Jesus' being—to manifest the nature and character of His Father. The great moment of glorification finally comes. And Jesus speaks of the falling and dying of a grain of wheat.

Now, if "being God" does not mean "something to take advantage of" but "emptying Himself," can 'being human' mean anything less? Are we surprised that Jesus says to the Greeks and to us in John 12:25, "Those who love their life lose it and those who hate their life in this world will keep it for eternal life." Jesus is telling us that if we cling to our lives, we destroy them. Why? Because clinging violates our essential nature and character. We were created in the image of God. That is, we were created

---

7. W. H. Vanstone, *The Stature of Waiting* (New York: Seabury Press, 1983), 72.

8. N. T. Wright

to reflect the nature and character of God, which means we are most fully human when we most faithfully copy the nature and character of God.

"Unless a grain of wheat falls into the ground and dies . . . " In Jesus we discover that God understands being God in terms of self-emptying love. Those who bear this God's image are most truly themselves when they empty themselves and give themselves away.

I am married to a woman who understands this better than anyone I know. I regularly stand in awe of Sharon: Giving herself away for our children and their friends, for me, for the students she mentors, for the children of the preschool . . . and radiating with joy as she does it! I have the graduate degree in theology . . . but next to her, I am, at best, in kindergarten. Sharon *gets* it. She understands that when Jesus calls us to "deny yourselves, take up your cross" He is not trying to squeeze us into an alien mold. Sharon understands that "lose your life" is a freedom word. And she understands that "lose your life" is not just for the season of Lent as though once Easter comes we can find a different mode of living. No, Sharon understands that Easter is not the end of the way of the cross. Easter is God's vindication of the way of the cross. Easter is God's "Yes" to the way of the grain of wheat.

"If it dies it bears much fruit." Cling to our lives, protect our own agendas and careers, insist that everything has to go our way, and we lose. We are violating who we were created and redeemed to be. Give our lives away and we win. We live by dying.

"Sir, we wish to see Jesus." We want to understand this remarkable Person who promises us life. It is the same request Moses made on Mount Sinai—"Yahweh, show me Your glory!"

Okay—now is the moment of glory. "The hour has come." *Now* you will see. *Now* you will see what being God is all about. *Now*

80

you will see the very heart of the universe—"If I be lifted up."
*Now* you will see discover the secret of the Kingdom of God.

"Unless a grain of wheat falls into the ground and dies, it abides by itself, alone. But if it dies it bears much fruit."

O King of Glory, grant us grace to live as gloriously as You!

CHAPTER SIX

# THE FINAL CONTRADICTION

*1 Corinthians 1:18-2:5*

Had we been there, on that Friday afternoon, when Jesus of Nazareth was hanging on a Roman cross, when the Carpenter from Galilee was being crucified, suffering the cruelest form of execution yet devised by human beings, would we have understood what was really happening?

We would, I think, have realized that "something extraordinary" was going on. The three hours of darkness at midday would have told us that. So would have the earth shaking and rocks splitting. We would, I think, have echoed, to one degree or another, the declaration made by the soldier standing guard: "Surely, this man was the Son of God." We would, I think, have realized that this Man was no ordinary Man and that this death was no ordinary death.

But would we have understood what was really happening? Would we have understood what the authors of the New Testament later came to understand and proclaim?

Would we have understood that the Man being crucified was the Lamb of God dying to take away the sin of the world?

Would we have understood that in this crucifixion God was reconciling Himself to the world?

Would we have understood that in the shedding of this Blood a New Covenant, a new agreement between God and humanity, was being sealed?

Would we have understood, as we saw in chapter one, that on this cross the Holy God was executing Holy wrath and executing it against Himself? That God Himself was saving us from Himself?

Would we have understood, as we saw in chapter two, that in this painful act the ransom was being paid to set us captives free?

Would we have understood, as we saw in chapter three, that in crying out, "My God, My God, why have You forsaken Me?" Jesus was taking up into Himself the separation sin deserves; that the separation from God we deserve was taken up by God into God so we never have to experience it?

Would we have understood, as we saw in chapter four, that in this death the principalities and powers were being disarmed? That the one who held the power of death was being rendered powerless by the Crucified One?

Would we have understood, as we saw in chapter five, that Jesus giving Himself on the cross was the ultimate expression of Divine glory?

No, we would not have understood. Not on our own. Never in a million years. Why? Because of 1 Corinthians 1:18-2:5:

For the word of the cross is to those who are perishing foolishness, but to us who are being saved it is the power of God. For it is written, "I will destroy the wisdom of the wise, and the cleverness of the clever I will set aside." Where is the wise man? Where is the scribe? Where is the debater of this age? Has not God made foolish the wisdom of the world? For since in the wisdom of God the world through its wisdom did not come to know God, God was well-pleased through the foolishness of the message preached to save those who believe. For indeed Jews ask for signs, and Greeks search for wisdom; we preach Christ crucified, to Jews a stumbling block, and to Gentiles foolishness, but to those who are the called, both Jews and Greeks, Christ the power of God and the wisdom of God. Because the foolishness of God is wiser than men, and the weakness of God is stronger than men.

For consider your calling, brethren, that there were not many wise according to the flesh, not many mighty, not many noble; but God has chosen the foolish things of the world to shame the wise, and God has chosen the weak things of the world to shame the things which are strong, and the base things of the world and the despised, God has chosen, the things that are not, that He might nullify the things that are, that no man should boast before God. But by His doing you are in Christ Jesus, who became to us wisdom from God, and righteousness and sanctification, and redemption, that, just as it is written, "Let him who boasts, boast in the Lord."

And when I came to you, brethren, I did not come with superiority of speech or of wisdom, proclaiming to you the testimony of God. For I determined to know nothing among you except Jesus Christ, and Him crucified. And I was with you in weakness and in fear and in much trembling. And my message and my preaching were not in persuasive words of wisdom, but in demonstration of the Spirit and of power, that your faith should not rest on the wisdom of men, but on the power of God.

We would not have understood what was happening at the cross because Christ crucified is a contradiction, the final

85

contradiction, of all human understanding of how the Living God relates to the world. More specifically, Christ crucified is the final contradiction of all human understanding of what it means for God to be the Savior of the world. Even more specifically, Christ crucified is the final contradiction of all human understanding of what it means for God to be God(!).

I say "final contradiction" because throughout history the Living God has said to humanity, "My thoughts are not your thoughts, neither are My ways your ways" (Isaiah 55:8).

At the cross, and in what Paul calls "the word of the cross (1 Corinthians 1:18), the age-long contradiction comes to a head. For the first-century world, be it Jewish or Gentile, the words "Christ" and "crucified" simply do not go together. "Christ crucified", "Messiah crucified" is an oxymoron. The word "Christ" implied power, might, and triumph. The word "crucified" implied weakness, humiliation, and defeat. As New Testament scholar Gordon Fee says, "'Christ crucified' is a contradiction in terms, of the same category as 'fired ice.'"[1]

To the Jewish mind, "Christ crucified" was not only a contradiction in terms; it was a stumbling block, or, as the word Paul uses literally means, a scandal, an offense. To the Gentile mind, "Christ crucified" was also not only a contradiction in terms; it was foolishness, or as the word Paul uses literally means, "utter nonsense," or in the words of the Roman historian Tacitus, "a perverse, extravagant superstition."[2]

But why? Why is "Christ crucified" the final contradiction?

I find it helps if we paraphrase the words of the text before us. In place of Paul's term "Jews," put the phrase, "the religious mind." And

---

1. Gordon Fee, *The First Epistle to the Corinthians* (Grand Rapids, Mich.: Eerdmans, 1987), 75.
2. Ibid., 76.

in place of Paul's term "Greeks," put the phrase, "the philosophical mind." And then ask: "Why does the 'religious mind' trip over the cross and find it so offensive? Why does the 'philosophical mind' laugh at the cross and find it so much nonsense?"

The word of the cross, Christ crucified, is an offense to the "religious mind" for two basic reasons.

First, the cross is so un-spectacular. The first-century Jews expected a Messiah who would come and overwhelm the world with dramatic, visible, "awesome" manifestations of strength and majesty. Paul says the religious folk sought "signs" (1:22), that is, powerful proofs. The religious folk expected the Messiah to validate Himself with dramatic miracles. Again and again they asked Jesus to give a "sign" (Matthew 12:38; 16:1, 4; Mark 8:11ff; John 6:30).

William Barclay, as usual, summarizes the historical situation so well.

> This very time during which Paul was writing produced a crop of false Messiahs, and all of them had beguiled the people into accepting them by promise of wonders. In AD. 45 a man called Theudas had emerged. He had persuaded thousands of people to abandon their homes and follow him out to the Jordan, by promising that, at his word of command, the Jordan would divide and he would lead them to dryshod across.
>
> In A.D. 54, a man from Egypt arrived in Jerusalem, claiming to be the Prophet. He persuaded thirty thousand people to follow him out to the Mount of Olives by promising that at his word command the walls of Jerusalem would fall down. That was the kind of thing that the Jews were of looking for. In Jesus they saw one who was meek and lowly, one who deliberately avoided the spectacular, one who served and ended on a cross, and it seemed to them an impossible picture of the Chosen One of God.[3]

---

3. William Barclay, *The Letters to the Corinthians* (Edinburgh: Saint

Now, we must be careful here. For Jesus did in fact do many wonders, many signs. So many so, says John, that "even the whole world would not have room for the books that would be written about them" (John 20:30). Jesus' deeds validated and manifested the truth of His Gospel, namely that in Him the Kingdom of God was breaking into the world. So it is right to ask Him to do such acts in our time. To heal, to restore, to recreate. That, after all, is what we are praying for when we pray, "Thy kingdom come on earth as it is in heaven." The problem was that the religious mind *demanded* such signs. A demand born not out of confidence in Jesus but out of skepticism. Demanding signs from God means demanding that God act on my terms; demanding that God be God according to my categories and presuppositions.

The cross is an offense because it is so sign-less, so power-less. How can such an un-spectacular, weak event be the saving act of God's Anointed?

The cross is an offense to the "religious mind" for a second reason. The Old Testament asserted that a man who hung on a tree—on a cross—was under a curse. In Deuteronomy 21:23 it says, "He that is hanged is accursed of God."

To the Jews of the first century the fact that Jesus hung on a cross did not make Him the Savior; it disproved the possibility altogether.[4] A crucified man was a cursed man. And a cursed man could hardly be God's Anointed, God's Christ. That is why Paul, before he met the Risen Jesus, was so enraged by the new "Nazarene sect," as he then called it. They were worshipping as God, One whom, on religious grounds, was cursed by God.

How then did Paul and other writers of the New Testament, who were also Jews, handle this scandal? They did not deny that

Andrews Press), 1956, 18.
    4.   Ibid., 17.

Jesus hung on a cross as a cursed man. They came to understand the mystery of the cross; namely that the curse Jesus bore was not His but ours (!). We had broken God's good law and consequently rightly stood under God's just curse. In his letter to the Galatians, Paul quotes from the Law: "Cursed is everyone who does not abide by all things written in the book of the law" (Galatians 3:10; Deut. 27:26).

And then Paul proclaims the wonder of the cross: "Christ redeemed us from the curse of the law, having become a curse for us—for it is written, 'Cursed be everyone who hangs on a tree'" (Galatians 3:13).

Paul saw in the cross a great exchange.

The "religious mind" saw only a part of the truth of the cross: Jesus hung as a cursed man. But the "religious mind" did not see the whole truth: Jesus had taken our place, becoming a curse for us!

The first-century Jewish rejection of "Christ crucified" illustrates the blinding power of religion and the blinding power of religious presuppositions. Many Jews of the first century, like many Jews, Buddhists, Hindus, and even Christians (!) of the our century, allowed their own theological categories to blind them to the presence and activity of God. They focused on only a part of the Old Testament witness to the Messiah—that of the victorious King. They ignored the part which spoke of a suffering Messiah (Isaiah 52:13-53:12). Therefore, when He came they did not recognize Him. And the message of the cross, instead of being the foundation stone of new life, became a stumbling block.

The "philosophical mind" laughed at the word of the cross. Why? For two basic reasons.

First, the philosophical mind of the first century was steeped in the thinking of Plato. Plato taught "truth and wisdom did not reside in particulars, but in universals."[5] A particular: a tree, a cat, a woman, only had meaning as it reflected the universal, the tree-ness, cat-ness, woman-ness. And here is the key point: One does not discover truth in particulars; truth is found only in the universals behind the particulars. Particulars have no inherent meaning. A bird has no inherent meaning; it has meaning only as an instance of bird-ness. "I" have no inherent meaning; "I" have meaning as an instance of man-ness.

You see then why the "word of the cross" was utter nonsense for Greeks and Romans. The "word of the cross" is radically particular. The "word of the cross" says that God has definitely acted on behalf of all humanity, indeed, on behalf of the whole universe, in one particular part of the planet, at one particular moment in history, in one particular Jewish man, in His particular birth, in His particular life, in His particular Death. "Nonsense," says the philosophical mind.

The circumstances of Jesus' death only made the message more laughable.[6] Socrates at least died with dignity, giving a treatise on life and death. Jesus died as a common criminal crying, "My God, My God, why have You forsaken Me?" That this particular death revealed the heart of God; that this particular death had any affect on any other person was a ridiculous and revolting idea to the philosophical mind. The philosopher judged Christians to be helplessly anti-intellectual for following and worshipping (!) a condemned criminal who died by the lowest form of execution.

---

5.    Michael Green, *Evangelism in the Early Church* (Grand Rapids, Mich.: Eerdmans), 2004, 69.

6.    Ibid., 70.

Such a particular event could not possibly have any ultimate, universal meaning.

Surprise! The cross effects a great reversal. Now the universals only have meaning as they relate to this one particular. "Love" now has meaning only as it relates to the love of the cross. "Justice" now has meaning only as it relates to the justice of the cross. "Holiness" now has meaning only as it relates to the holiness of the cross. "Human-ness" now has meaning only as it relates to the Human on the cross. And (!) "God-ness" now has meaning only as it relates to the God on the cross.

This leads us to the second reason the "philosophical mind" laughed at the word of the cross. Greeks and Romans held, as axiomatic, as invisible law, that the gods do not and cannot suffer.

The Greeks and Romans affirmed a number of attributes of the gods: all-powerful, all-knowing, etc. But the first and foremost attribute exalted was *"apatheia,"* from which we get the English word "apathy". However, the word *"apatheia"* meant more than we mean by apathy. It meant that the gods were incapable of feeling. If there was only one God, that God would be incapable of feeling. The gods, simply because they are gods, are unaffected by human sin and misery. If the gods could in any way feel our pain it would mean, according to the Greeks, that we humans can affect the gods. This would mean, according to the Greeks, that the gods were no longer gods. Thus, the highest attribute of divinity: *apatheia.* So, too, in Buddhism and in much New Age philosophy.

See why the word of the cross was sheer folly, perverse superstition, to some people? The One, True, Living God incarnate in Christ . . . feeling? God suffering? "Nonsense!" To the Greek mind there was no way that one who suffered the way Jesus suffered had any relation to the true God.

Surprise, surprise! The philosophers of the first century, and in the centuries since, overlooked a fundamental attribute of God. They overlooked the freedom of God. It is the Christian philosopher Jürgen Moltmann, having suffered through the horror of the Nazi Holocaust, who has shown that the philosophers, then and now, never considered the possibility that the One, True God, might freely choose to open Himself up to the pain of the world. The philosophical mind never considered that out of deep love for humanity the One, True, Living God might freely choose to suffer for and with humanity.[7] They never considered the possibility that in freedom God can break out of philosophical boxes.

O the wonderful "word of the cross!" The God who supposedly cannot suffer does! The God who supposedly remains aloof from human misery came into the misery and made it His own, and then suffered more deeply than any human being ever had or ever will. No suffering is unknown to the Center of Reality. As Dorothy Sayers, the English mystery writer once said, "whatever game God is playing with the universe He is Man enough to play by the rules." Not that she thought God was playing a game; just that the One, True, God has chosen to enter into the wreckage and make it His own. God chooses to suffer.

And God's suffering is what gives God credibility to a suffering world. The poem, "Jesus of the Scars," written by Edward Shillito after the brutality of World War I, says it well:

> If we have never sought Thee, we seek Thee now.
> Thine eyes burn through the dark, our only stars;

---

7. Jürgen Moltmann, *The Trinity and The Kingdom* (Minneapolis: Augsburg, 1984), p. 23.

We must have the sight of thorn-pricks on Thy brow,
We must have Thee, O Jesus of the Scars.
The heavens frighten us; they are too calm;
In all the universe we have no place;
Our wounds are hurting us; where is the balm?
Lord Jesus, by Thy scars, we claim Thy grace.
The other gods were strong; but Thou was weak;
They rode, but Thou didst stumble to a throne;
But to our wounds only God's wounds can speak,
And not as a god has wounds, but Thou alone.[8]

Christ crucified: The final contradiction. To the "religious mind," an offense. To the "philosophical mind," nonsense. But to those who are called, both Jews and Greeks, Christ crucified, the power of God and the wisdom of God. For in the foolishness and weakness of the cross, God has done what human wisdom and power could never do.[9]

Now, the implications of this for our everyday living are staggering. There are at least two.

First, we are now better equipped to share the Gospel, the Good News, with our contemporaries. Why? Before we share, we know that the word of the cross is initially unpalatable.[10] We know before we share that the word of the cross is initially offensive or ridiculous. So we can relax. We can simply share the Gospel as it is and trust the contradiction to do its work. The Gospel steps on the toes of all who think they are wise and strong. The French sociologist Jacques Ellul reminds us that grace is odious to us. On first hearing, grace offends. The Good

---

8. Quoted by David Smith, *Mission Beyond Christendom* (London, 2003) 31.

9. C. K. Barrett, *A Commentary on the First Epistle to the Corinthians* (London: A. & C. Black, 1971), 56.

10. Ralph Martin, *1 Corinthians-Galatians* (London: Scripture Union, 1978), 1.

News of the cross offends the wise, for the cross says we cannot find God in our wisdom; God has come to us in "foolishness." The Good News of the cross offends the strong, for the cross says we cannot redeem ourselves in our own power; God has come to us in weakness. Beneath the cross no one can boast (1 Corinthians 1:28-29). No one can pat herself on the back for finding God. No one can pat himself on the back for redeeming himself.

Sooner or later we have to come to terms with the "offense" and "nonsense" of the cross. And then we have to resist the temptation to make it less offensive. We have to let the scandal stand; to let the folly stand. To try to remove the final contradiction, as the Church has regularly done, is to subvert the Gospel. And a subverted Gospel is finally no Gospel at all. It becomes only good advice, but not Good News.

We are to let the Gospel stand as it is: God's wisdom in "foolishness"; God's power in "weakness." That was the apostle Paul's strategy in Corinth, a city proud of its "wisdom" and "power." He told the Corinthians, "I determined to know nothing among you except Jesus Christ and Him crucified" (2:2). For he was confident that the foolish and weak message of the "foolish" and "weak" God finally wins people. It won me.

The second implication of embracing the final contradiction is more critical. The contradiction frees us to live the new and different life to which the Crucified Lord calls us. At first glance, indeed (!) at second, third, tenth glance, the way of Jesus Christ appears weak and foolish.

"If someone slaps you on the right cheek, give him the other also" (Matthew 5:39). Weakness!! "If someone wants to sue you for your shirt, let him take your coat, too" (5:40). Foolishness!! "If someone forces you to go one mile, go two" (5:41). You've got to be kidding! "Pray for those who persecute you" (5:44). Grant them the same privilege you have, to stand beneath the cross and be forgiven. "Love your enemies" (5:44). Seek the welfare of your enemies with the same zeal with which you seek your own. What?! "Deny yourself and take up your cross" (Mark 8:34). "If you try to save your life you will lose it; lose your life for My sake"...give yourself away in servant-love and you will find it. Utter folly!

On that cross that Friday, the "foolishness" of God accomplished what the wisdom of humanity never could; on that cross the "weakness" of God accomplished what the power of humanity never could. In light of that cross we now know that "wisdom" which does not lead us in the way of the Crucified is ultimately foolishness; we know that "power" which does not act as the Crucified is ultimately weakness. And we can gladly accept the charge that we are fools, as Paul says, "fools for Christ's sake" (1 Corinthians 4:10).

So, how should we respond today to this final contradiction? Paul makes an arresting claim. To those who are on their way to destruction (1:18), Christ crucified is foolishness and weakness. But to those who are, by the grace of God, on their way to salvation (1:18), Christ crucified is the wisdom and power of God. And we say with Isaac Watts:

> Forbid it Lord, that I should boast,
> Save in the death of Christ my God.
> All the vain things that charm me most,
> I sacrifice them to His blood.
>
> Were the whole realm of nature mine,
> That were a present far too small.
> Love so amazing, so Divine,
> Demands my life, my soul, my all.

# SUGGESTED READING

The following books are suggested for moving into greater understanding of the saving death of Jesus of Nazareth.

Gustav Aulen, *Christus Victor* (New York: MacMillan, 1969).

Richard Bauckham, *God Crucified* (Grand Rapids: Eerdmans, 1998).

Henri Blocher, *Evil and the Cross* (Vancouver, BC: Regent College Publishing, 2003).

Martin Hengel, *Crucifixion: In the Ancient World and the Folly of the Message of the Cross* (Philadelphia: Fortress Press, 1977).

Alister E. McGrath, *The Mystery of the Cross* (Grand Rapids, Michigan: Academie Books, 1988).

Jürgen Moltmann, *The Crucified God* (New York: Harper & Row, 1974).

Leon Morris, *The Apostolic Preaching of the Cross* (Grand Rapids, Michigan: Eerdmans, 1955).

Richard John Neuhaus, *Death on a Friday Afternoon: Meditations on The Last Words of Jesus from the Cross* (New York: Basic Books, 2000).

J. I. Packer, *Knowing God* (Downers Grove: Inter Varsity Press, 1976).

John R. W. Stott, *The Cross of Christ* (Downers Grove: IVP, 1986).

N. T. Wright, *Jesus and the Victory of God* (Minneapolis: Fortress, 1996).